Dating Advice For Men: Discover What Women Want & Become An Alpha Male Who Easily Attracts & Seduces Women

Buyer Bonus

I want to thank you for your purchase of this book. As a way of extending my thanks I am offering a **free** dating course and two ebooks.

The course is, Attract Women: The Simple Strategy to Attract Women will help you to realize your dating goals much quicker. Whilst the two books, **The Confident New You** & **Make Her Chase You** will help you gain more confidence and success with women.

Here's just a tiny fraction of what you'll discover:

- Smooth ways to ask the girl for her number and have amazing dates, relationships and mind blowing sex.
- Build a lifestyle that will guarantee you success with women
- Where to easily meet women in your city
- How to Look and Feel Your Best
- Keep the conversation going, without appearing awkward
- How to confidently express yourself and captivate attention
- And much more about confidence, relationships and dating

So if you're looking for a simple way to attract women and have more confidence then:

Free, Sign Me Up

- Introduction
- Chapter Alpha Male code
- Inner game
- Outer Game
- Female Psychology
- Attractive Communication
- Where to Meet Women
- Night Game
- Day Game
- Job Game
- Social Circle Game
- Online Game
- Tinder
- Other Dating Sites and Applications
- Texting
- Dates
- Sex
- Relationships
- Conclusion

Foreword: Shanghai 2019

This foreword details a story to inspire your journey. I have written it not to impress you. But to impress upon you that you too can make massive changes in your dating life using the knowledge in this book. Read it if you wish or skip ahead to the actionable steps in the chapters after it.

Saturday nights are always fun, but this one will be hard to beat. The sun was setting over the Bund in central Shanghai. Room service sent me up some green tea as I prepared for a headline DJ show at one of the top local clubs. The crowd in Shanghai was always crazy and so I prepared for a wild night. The after party would be much wilder...

Midnight approached and with my set ready to rock I passed some time browsing the local single ladies on the latest dating application, Tantan.

Swipe, pass, swipe, pass, pass, swipe, match, match…..Super like, hmmm this girl looks pretty hot. Abigail, rich, young and a fairly famous actress. Absolutely gorgeous. She texted me first.

"Hey, nice to meet you, I'm Abi"
"Likewise, call me Darcy"

We talked for a while, sending each other voice notes and chit chat.

"I saw your poster for the show tonight."
"Yeah you should come."

At this point I could tell she was really into me. Years of learning to become an alpha male had taught me this skill. She confirmed my thoughts.

"I booked a vip table."
"Great will see you there."

Ring, ring, the hotel room phone rang "Your taxi is ready Mr Carter". I strolled downstairs to be greeted by the driver. "Welcome Mr Carter" The Mercedes door opened and I relaxed into the soft leather seats as we navigated our way through the streets of Shanghai towards Club Modu.

Red carpets were rolled out, pretty girls stood with flowers and wide smiles. Photographers lined up to take pictures of me as I entered the club. I stopped to take a few selfies with some of the fans and signed a couple of posters. Big basslines rumbled my stomach and flashes stunned my eyes as I entered the club. It was like a colosseum of nightlife with the DJ in the middle conducting the club. Glitzy champagne girls twirled for customers and toned athletic women grinded on the stage.

To my left, there she was. Elegantly posed in the VIP area. Guards stood by to protect her. Porcelain white skin, flawless, a perfect body and juicy breasts. From across the room we made eye contact. I approached her with a slight smile.

"I'm Abi," she said as she extended her hand.
I took her hand gently squeezing it. "Great to meet you"
"Madam your table is ready" The waiter announced as the guards escorted us to her table. There she had ordered and already paid for six bottles of the finest champagne. The minimum bottle charge her was two hundred and fifty USD.

"You look much better in real life" she whispered into my ear. I squeezed her hips with my whole hand and gave her a confident smile. The crowd was electric and she was on fire. We talked for a while, reclining back into the plush semicircular sofas of a VIP table. One more cheers and a warm hug before I went on stage. "Good luck" she wished me as I made my way to the stage.

I proceeded to the main stage and laid down a killer set. Hands waved in the air, bottles popped and lights flashed as I captivated the club. Abi danced seductively on top of the sofas, watching me intently. Guys tried to approached but were all ignored. Later she joined a table of friends. My set finished and I joined them.

"Make love to me tonight," she says as she pulls me into her arms.

"Of course, where are you staying?" "The Ritz Carlton."

The words were like jewels dripping of her silk tongue and rose lips. The Ritz Carlton, one of the most prestigious hotels in Shanghai. "One more drink and then we go." I told her. We danced some more. Then I lead her out of the club and past the big boss who gives me an approving nod.

Outside it's raining so I lift my coat over us and take the short walk across the street to her hotel. Grandiose would be a minor statement for this hotel, the lobby looked like something out of a Gatsby movie.

"I'm staying at the penthouse suite, is that ok?" she asks me. "Sure" I reply. Confident all the time.

We take the lift upstairs, and open the double doors to the suite. A huge white king size bed with plush pillows and duvet awaits. I throw her onto it. "Fuck me now" she says. We tear each others clothes off, I pull down her panties and thrust into her. "Harder" she tells me as I proceed to marathan fuck her on the bed and then down onto the dining area. I pull out and finish on her perfect breasts. We rest for a short while and then make long lustrous sex for another two hours before falling into eachohters arms asleep.

Vvvv, vvvvv, I awake to a vibrating sound the next day. She hits the snooze button. "What time is your flight?" I ask. "It's ok I will book a new one" and pulls me into her for a kiss. We sleep in some more.

We wake up and talk about her life. She works in movies, fashion and modelling. Often she has to travel which is why she was in Shanghai.

"It can get lonely" she tells me. "I understand" She tells me she loves sex but rarely goes out so she travels with this boyfriend. "Boyfriend?" I ask her. "Yes" she replies as she pulls out this small egg shaped thing.

She switches it on and it starts vibrating. I watched her play with herself as I caress her breasts and kiss her. Her body shakes as she comes to a climax. She lays back smiles.

"Have you ever had a threesome?" she asks. "Yes, but with girls only" I tell her. "I want to try" she replies. "Would you like to try with me" I ask her. She nods and laughs.

Last time I was in Shanghai I hooked up with this cute student. Katherine a cute nineteen year with a tight body and a peachy ass. We had some dynamite sex and I remember her asking me if I wanted to have a threesome. I show her pics to Abi…"hmmm nice text her". I text Katherine with some catch up texting and then throw in the hook.

"Hey, remember when you asked me if I wanted a threesome?"
"Yeah"
"I'm with someone now at the Ritz, she's really hot. Wanna come over?"
"Sure."
"OK bring condoms."

Katherine arrives. We ordered room service, open some wine and chat a little. I let the girls get to know each other whilst I sit back and relax. Outside it's raining, what a great place to be right now. Inside the penthouse of the Ritz Carlton, two babes, room service on tap. The life.

"Let's take a bath" I suggest.
"Sure" They reply.

The marble decorated bathroom has an extra large bathtub, warm and soapy for all of us. We sit in there together, kiss a little, and laugh a lot. "Your going to feel like a king" Abi tells me as I smile. This feeling is really like a King. we soak for a while then I lead them to the bed.

"Show her your toy" I tell Abi. She takes out the egg vibrator and gives to Katherine who goes down on her at the same time. Abi is laying on my chest, holding my dick and making out with me. I'm soaking in the moment. I Strip them naked and bang them both, switching it up as I feel. We bang every each way with me climaxing on both of them as they make out with each other. We have about three more sessions in between food breaks and talking. All day, what an epic day!

But it wasn't always like this.....

I was born to a normal working class family in the mid eighties. My parents have been married since I was a kid. Growing up my life was pretty standard. I did OK with girls up until I was about sixteen when I moved away from the city to rural life. My family had some issues during this time. My older brother passed away and I fell into a deep depression.

From the age of sixteen to twenty one I got laid twice with two very average girls. Poor results from a poor attitude. The fog of my depression started to lift when I went to university. But it was still there in the background.

At university I met Laura. We had a three year relationship but towards the end of it I pushed her away. At the back of my mind I felt there was unfinished business inside of me. That I was a caged animal who wanted to sow his seeds around the world. But I didn't have the balls to end it, I let it stagnate. Laura ended it for me.

The break up destroyed me. I was depressed and lonely for a long time. Out of desperation I searched for some books to help me. To my amazement people had broken down dating into something you could learn. They talked about approaching girls, how to talk to them, dates, relationships and sex. I started to implement the knowledge.

I will never forget the first time I got laid from that knowledge. Driving back from a girls apartment in Prague. I watched the sunrise over Charles Bridge inspired that it had worked. I revised the knowledge into my own system from testing and rehearsing it. This inspired me to quit my bullshit job and move to the other side of the world. This got me laid like a king. This got me the hottest chicks, love and peak experiences in my life.

I have slept with millionaire business owners, Hollywood actresses, Playboy models, threesomes, FHM number one models, catwalk models, webcam girls, girls next door and much more.

You see I tell you this story not to impress you but to inspire you that where I came from living experiences like this is a miracle. A miracle that is based on a skillset that you too can learn. This book can do the same for you, if your ready.

The Alpha Male Code

To begin this journey we need to find out your purpose in life. A man with a strong sense of self purpose who is going after his goals is highly attractive to women. In fact, most women will find that broke guy who is hustling his way yet having a purpose way more attractive than some complacent rich guy. The pursuit of goals is the pursuit of happiness.

To become an alpha male you need a vision for your life. Your life needs to be about more than women. That might sound counterintuitive to you but believe me women will be more turned on by your independence. If your goal and purpose in life is a woman than you will act needy and be a wreck of emotions. That is completely unattractive.

Consider the areas of your life.

Happiness
- What do you want to do to become happier?
- Meditation, a retreat, books?
- Is there anything else important to your happiness?

Health
- What kind of body do you want?
- What do you want to try?
- Is there anything else important to your health?

Money
- How much money do you want to earn each month?
- How do you want to earn it?
- How much money do you want saved?
- Is there anything else important to your wealth?

Relationships
- What kind of woman you want?

Be specific as possible here. There is more to a woman than just physical attractiveness. Of course for most of use that's number one but you need to consider other aspects besides her looks.

Do you like smart girls? Do you look party girls? Are you looking for older or younger women? Petite or tall? Make a list of all the qualities you like and it will help you to find those women and also screen out any that don't fit.
- What kind of relationship you want?

Open, casual, wife? Relationships will be discussed in more detail in the relationship chapter. If you would like to refer to that please skip ahead to that chapter.
- Is there anything else important to your relationships?

Career
- What are your career goals?
- What is your dream job?
- Is there anything else important to your career?

Travel and Adventure
- Where do you want to travel to?
- What adventurous things do you want to try?
- Is there anything else important to you here?

Lifestyle
- Where do you want to live?
- What material things do you want to own?
- Is there anything else?

Social
- Who do you want to know?
- What kind of social life do you want?
- Is there anything else?

Giving
- Who can you help?
- How can you help?
- Is there anything else important to you here?

Brainstorm each of these areas. Think big and dare yourself to dream. This can take as long as you want. I suggest an hour a day for a month or so. Try writing them down every morning and then collate the results.

When you have come up with a detailed list start to categorize it by the goals you expect to reach in one year, three years and five years or more. Then prioritize your most important ones for the year. List all the actions you need to take, people that can help you and so on. When your happy with that then you can keep it in a file which you can look at each day. Review your progress and actions often.

Values

Values influence your life in a profound way. Values affect the decisions we make. Therefore we need to be aware that we are living in harmony with our values. What are your values?

To discover your values think about five people who you admire. They can be famous or people you personally know. Write down five values you that you think each of them have. For example:

- Bruce Lee - health, mastery, learning, success, family
- Barack Obama - knowledge, giving, community, wealth, leading

When you have a list of twenty five values choose five to ten that resonate the most with you. Write a sentence about each and look at these everyday. If you want to take it further do what Benjamin Franklin did and every week ask yourself if you lived according to these values. This will help to ground you as an alpha male.

Outcome Independence

Outcome independence is one of the most important components to master towards becoming an alpha male and attracting women. In essence outcome independence is not caring about how things turn out.

See a hot girl don't care, approach her. There never is going to be a right time, so just do it. If you feel like everyone is watching you realise that most people are distracted by their own lives that they won't realize or pay attention. Be the player not the spectator. It's better to face your fears and reap the rewards than cower and think what if.

She doesn't text you back. Move on, nothing really matters. Outcome independence will set you apart from the pack.

Now this is not to say that you should not give a damn about your life, acting yolo and allowing it to screw up. Absolutely not, long term and overall your vision should be very outcome dependent. How you view your goals and mission in life is going to be very outcome dependent. But the small and individual things such as specific people and events in life is what you need to let go of control of. This will make you highly attractive to women.

The alpha male is confident that long term he will reach his goals. If you desire results from the big picture and let go of desiring specific outcomes from particular singular events then you will become outcome dependent.

Inner Game

Everything begins in the mind. Inner game is primarily about raising your self esteem. Without a good level of self esteem/self love you will feel less of a man and not worthy of being around attractive women or approaching them. Self esteem is a term used in psychology to describe the overall sense of selse worth or value of a person. It can be thought of as how much you like and appreciate yourself. There are some techniques and tools you can use to increase your self esteem. This is critical to your success with women. Feel good and good things will happen. We need to present the best version of ourselves.

Affirmations

Affirmations might seem a bit woo, woo and out there to you but it's been proven that they can subconsciously raise your self esteem. This will turn you into a driven and powerful alpha male. Try saying affirmations to yourself every morning and night. In front of the mirror is great. I usually say mine in the elevator, it's my habitual trigger.

Affirmations should be phrased in the present tense and consist of the things you aspire to be. Come up with your own. For example.

"I am an alpha male"
"I am attractive and confident"

"I am always attracting gorgeous women into my life"
"I am fearless"

Mindset

How do you think about yourself? The way you think about yourself is projected onto the women you meet. If your thinking things like:

"Oh god I'm such a loser, hopefully she accepts me".
"I'm so unlucky with women".

These stories that we tell ourselves are not helping us. They are insidious and will destroy our results. Wouldn't it be much better if we thought things like.

"I'm such a boss, she is gonna be so amazed. Just wait"
"She is so lucky to be in the presence of me"

I know what your thinking...but what if my life sucks? Well you need to reframe it because it's all about perception. Let's take a look at some examples.

- You haven't got laid in six months or more and your mindset:

"I just wish a girl would like me for who I am"

Reframe that to:

"These girls need to up their game and try harder"

"I'm on my pathway to the hottest chicks, right now and I am 100% in charge."

"I'm working on becoming the best version of myself, average girls will not do"

Lets try some more examples:

- Your twenty seven years old and still living with your mom and dad.

Reframe that to:

"I'm a well balanced man who values his family."

"I'm on a journey to becoming an alpha one day I will look back on these challenges and be grateful for them."

Weed out the negatives and focus on the positives. Anytime you have a negative thought, write it down. Do this and notice the bullshit you tell yourself. Believe that you can be with any girl you want. You are the prize. Master yourself.

Sources of Positivity

On a subconscious and conscious level we need to be aware of what influences us. We are so influenced by the smallest things. Analyze your daily activities and the people that you regularly encounter. Is it helping you become a better person? Are they the kind of people that you aspire to be?

Cut out the TV, netflix and rubbish on social media. Replace it with positive things like, reading, being social and exercising. Cut out the negative people in your life. Even if it means being alone. If your working in some lame job then have a plan to get out of it. If the people there suck then retreat to some positive talks on Youtube, audiobooks and so on.

Cut out pornography. I don't condone the use of it. However, contrary to the nofap movement it does have some value. For one it can give you inspiration and ideas. For two it will help you control urges to sleep with average girls. Then on a negative moving away force it will give you a feeling of pity to make things happen for real. If you do use porn, save it for the end of the day. Ideally watch it once a week. Keep it to softcore material. Other than that, use your mind to get off.

Finally avoid any gossip. That includes about people you don't know. Resist the urge. If people do it. Don't engage. Walk away or remain neutral. Only say things that you would feel comfortable saying to their face. Also no lying. Keep your mind positive. If you have negativity in your life use it as a motivation to change.

Morning Routine

Morning routines are a bit of a buzz word these days. But with good reason. Many of the most successful people in the world have morning routines. It's the foundation of your day and will help you stay grounded as an alpha male.

Here is an overview of my morning routine. I stick to this most days. Some days are better than others of course and not every morning is going to be perfect. But if you can keep stacking those wins and start winning the day then your well on your way to more success with women.

Focus on mastering each of the following. If you don't have time, wake up earlier or drop things that don't resonate with you. The following should take from forty five minutes to one hour.

1. Smile
The first thing I like to do is to begin my day with a smile. The alarm goes off and i immediately smile. No snoozing. Start the day with the intent of positivity.

2. Write out goals
Next to my bed I have a notepad and pen. I write out my top goals and three things I am grateful for. This will help to set your focus for the day.

3. Brush teeth
Next get out of bed and brush your teeth. This is an action of self love and respect. Be good to yourself.

4. Meditate

I've tried various forms of meditation over the years and the subject is way too huge to put into a paragraph. But in short, I find that twenty minutes of meditation is best. Focus on your breathing. When thoughts come observe them but do not engage in them. Eyes can be open or closed. Sit up straight or cross legged. Remain still.

5. Prayer and Affirmations

After meditation I say a short prayer to thank God for bringing me here, for the values I have and for my family and any other things I am grateful for. Those would be my key goal areas, health, wealth, love, happiness, and success. I then say aloud my top affirmations. I also repeat these during the day when I get chance. You can also take this time to forgive anyone you have conflict with.

6. Read

I will usually read for about ten minutes whilst I have a coffee or breakfast. Read good books, no checking social media. I also read my goals and information from the last week of my goals review.

7. Yoga

Now it's time for some yoga to wake up the body. I like ten minutes or more if there is time. I also add in some martial arts training. Up to you if you want to. There is time if you make it.

8. Shower

You should be nicely warmed up by now. Take a shower. During the shower i often ask myself key questions. Such as what am I grateful for, how does that make me feel. What am I happy about? What do I love? Who do i love?

9. First task of the day
You should be fired up for an amazing day! Get out there and meet some women.

With the morning routine you can take some of the things in there and do them again during the day. Maybe you take a nap and want to restart. Or you could use some to pump yourself up before a gaming session. At the end of the day you should journal your results and add in some meditation or things to relax you.

Journaling

On your journey towards becoming better with women and becoming an alpha male you should be taking notes and journaling. This can be in handwritten form or digital format. Writing by hand is good for dealing with emotional issues and setting goals.

When your starting out your going to have to face a lot of your demons. Write them down in great detail and don't censor yourself. Even the darkest secrets of your soul. Let them out and be liberated from them.

After each interaction with a girl write down what was good, bad and what you need to improve upon. This works well as a digital note since you can file it and keep coming back to those particular sticking points. Over time you will certainly improve. In a few years you will look back on those notes and be amazed at how far you have come. Spend the time to make notes and write down the things you learn. Every week organize those notes and take action on them.

Outer Game

What kind of life are you living? Is it exciting? Are you inspired to get out of bed everyday?

If your just waking up, going to work then coming home and crashing out on the sofa do you think that is appealing or attractive to women? To become more attractive to women you need to fix up your lifestyle and outer game.

Make some plans to travel. Join some clubs and social activities. Take hikes in nature. Go swimming, go for a massage, watch interesting movies, hang out in fancy coffee shops and so on. Diversify your life and make it interesting. Personally I aim to travel to a new country once a month sometimes with girls I am dating. I also am involved in the gym, sports, coffee shops and movies.

Make sure you have adequate resources to be dating women. You don't need to be rich but being able to support yourself helps. If your really broke you can still get laid but you will need to be more creative. Considering things such as going on dates to cheap or free places and being careful with transportation.

Now, let's look at some of the outer game elements to help you become more attractive to women.

Clothes

If your dressing like a bum or still wearing the same clothes from five years ago then it's going to hurt your chances of meeting quality women. Good clothes can turn an average looking man into a handsome guy. Here are some tips for finding clothes that will make you look great.

- Check out celebrities and models who look similar to you. What do they wear? Find something similar.
- Match your skin tone with colors that compliment it.
- Always choose clothes that fit great and make you look awesome. No maybes.
- Get some good shoes to match your outfits
- Buy some great looking gym clothes. Wear some cool joggers and a fashionable tank top that shows off your figure.
- Buy some accessories that tell a story. This could be a cheap bracelet from a buddhist temple you visited. Or a pendent from your grandfather. Also if you have tattoos build a backstory around them. All of this is mysterious and attractive.
- Go shopping with girls you find attractive and ask for their opinion.

Grooming

Fix up and look sharp. Every moment of the day you must present your best self. Women are sensitive to grooming and it will make you more attractive to them whilst making you feel more confident. Here is a checklist of things you need to consider.

- Shower
- Fresh breath
- Hair styled
- Smelling good

If your at the gym some of those things might not be possible. But you can always calibrate your approaches by saying something like "Sorry I'm a bit sweaty I just had a big workout". In fact I often approach girls at the gym and they find that attractive. At the very least you should have some decent gym clothes. Again make sure your hair and breath are on point.

Apartment & Logistics

A guy with amazing logistics, average looks and poor game will get laid way more than a handsome guy with amazing game but poor logistics. If you live right next to a venue where hot girls go then closing them will be so much easier. If you like certain girls then move to where they are.

Make it happen, move as close to the hub of girls you like as possible. It's better to get a smaller apartment in the centre than some fancy place far away. Girls will easily come somewhere that is just five minutes away rather than thirty minutes or more.

When it comes to your apartment make sure it is clean, smelling good and has some character. Adding character will give her things to talk about and make her feel comfortable. This could be things such as background music, pictures, pets and so on.

When she is in your apartment make her feel as comfortable as possible. Have some alcohol and music prepared. Put on some YouTube videos in the background. There should be plenty of stimulation so that she is not feeling uncomfortable. Don't just bring her to a place with just a bed and some poor lighting.

In addition to your apartment good logistics consists of having some great dating venues near to your place. You need a couple of places that you can take your dates to that are nearby. This makes moving to a close very easy. Find some cool little bars or coffee shops nearby that you can meet for your first dates. Even better if you have some fun things such as bowling or swimming nearby. More on that later.

What Do Women Want?

The age old question men ask themselves. Because if we knew, we would be happy to give it to them! What you really need to ask yourself is. Are you giving the women in your life real value or chasing for something from them?

Do they actually want what you have to offer or are you just another guy trying to get a quick bang? Give them something they can really value deep down in their mind. Know what women really value in a man and you will have great dating success.

So what do women really value in men? Pay attention here, this is the most important chapter. Let's begin with the initial attraction.

Physical Attractiveness

Physical attractiveness differs between men and women. Men are stimulated easily by physical attractiveness. But for women it includes much more than you would think. This includes, the way you present yourself through fashion, grooming, body language, tonality, eye contact, health and so on. Then there is your assumed amount of resources and social status which includes other women she assumes are attracted to you.

The good news is that you can start improving on them right away. The story begins with initial attraction. Get your foot in the door by being physically attractive as best you can. It will improve your chances with her. Then that's where the attraction stages and falling in love begins.

Attraction

Self Respect

Self respect is the first of four elements which causes women to fall in love. Her initial interest in you already has high internal value to her. Self respect is conveyed through your actions and personality but it is not something that should not be confused with arrogance. There is a key difference between the two. Arrogance is about being better than other people and is achieved by lowering their value against yours. Authentic self respect doesn't compare against others. Simply it equates to "I'm awesome, no comparisons, just awesome, period"

Women are implicitly attracted to authentic inner belief. What you feel they feel. Plus when you behave in harmony with your beliefs it all becomes positively self reinforced. There are some great ways to demonstrate self respect.

Qualification

Never do things to seek approval from women. As a man who values himself you will have specific criteria that you look for in women. Screen women for these criteria but do it without trying to act better than anyone. Most guys have zero standards so the very fact that you challenge her and ask her engaging questions will convey that you have high standards. These should be things that don't involve her looks. Such as. Is she smart? Does she work out? What's important to you in a woman?

Ask qualifying questions which encourage her to explain what's better about her instead of all the other women out there. Discover what makes her unique. For example ask her:

"What's the best thing about you?" or
"What's something you are most proud of?"

Maintain your attractive position. You're the one giving approval here. Be the buyer not the seller. If she shares anything personal have empathy and never put her down or be rude. If you disagree with her about something simple or silly you can disagree in a humorous way.

Pausing is a powerful way to show self respect. When a woman talks, pause before you reply. It shows your confidence and also encourages her to continue talking about herself. She will sense that you are not feeling pressured to fill any silences. In turn this builds comfort and attraction with you. Let her talk more than you. This will increase her investment in you which should always be more than your investment in her. Comfort her to reveal more about herself. Ask open questions and dig deeper into her responses.

Make the decisions wherever you can and be the person that's in control. Instead of asking questions you need to be leading and suggesting things. This is why men in positions of power often have many women chasing them. Bar managers, business owners and so on. Outside of those it's very important that in your interactions with her you present yourself as being a leader.

Internal Strength

The second thing a woman is attracted to is internal strength. This is your power to stand up for yourself and disagree or say no if necessary. This might sound counterintuitive but when a woman knows that you are fine to leave her then she will be much more attracted to you.

For example, if you don't like certain behaviors or things she does then tell her. If she is always texting when she is around you then tell her. Be strong and grounded with your boundaries set. She will respect you for it.

Respect her view and opinion at the same time but be able to stand up for yourself if she challenges your beliefs. Through this she will begin to notice that you could be a man with internal strength that she could trust more. You don't need to be fighting battles all the time. Most of the time the small stuff doesn't matter.

Deal with her tests

Women are constantly testing men to see if they are going to be a good match for them. This occurs mostly on a subconscious level as part of her biological wiring. As a man you need to be aware of her tests. A man with internal strength reacts to tests with indifference. When she challenges you on any area of your life, shrug it off and be indifferent. If she mocks you just laugh it off and take it as a compliment. When you first start dating a woman, avoid doing any big favors for her. After a few months you can help her a bit more. But at the start you don't want to be friendzoned or some guy that does stuff for her.

Status

Status in essence is when a woman believes that other women on her level or above her's are also attracted to you. This can be a hard concept for guys to understand because again it's counter intuitive. If you see a hot girl surrounded by men in a bar your probably thinking she is slut or something along those lines. But if a woman sees a man surrounded by women in bar she is wired to find him more attractive. For men the effect is not the same.

Now women do have the same requirements in a partner as men do, health, fertility, and good genes. They just determine if a man has those in a different way. When it appears that other women already want you then it makes sense to her because you have already succeeded the criteria for women on her level or above. Essentially you have Status.

Make use of this cognitive bias. Imagine you had five or more women on her level or above chasing you. How would you behave? Would you be more relaxed and less outcome dependent? Would it matter how long she took to reply to you texts? Would your standards be higher? Behave as if you have complete abundance and it will manifest in your life. She will feel that and become more attracted to you.

Now if you struggle with that concept then you can cultivate a life of abundance in other areas of your life first. For example if you have a lot of success in business let that act as a Status mindset for you. Use it as a pillar of strength allowing you to behave as if you are an attractive man with unlimited options.

All of this also works if your in a relationship. Maybe the spark has died out. Reignite her interest with Status. You can say simple things like "this new girl at work asked me out" or "the Dr told me I was handsome today". Then move on like it means nothing.

Challenge

One of the most powerful elements of dating which allows you to level up with wealthier, cooler and better looking men is challenge. Any man can make use of it but many don't because like most dating advice it is counterintuitive and goes against your own instincts.

This does not mean being aloof or looking down on women. Essentially it means that your not easy. When you present yourself as a challenge it is highly attractive because women love to chase a man. Instead of always texting her, create space and make her chase you. When she wins your attention it validates her attraction for you.

Pulling/complimenting and only pushing/putting down or challenging her on their own are both unattractive behaviors. Use the concept of push and pull to influence her attraction for you. The key to push pull is to mix it up. Compliment her sometimes, and challenge her sometimes. When you do it be playful. Say something like:

"It's really a shame, that I don't find you attractive" said with a playful smile.

"Your cute...like my kid sister"

Give women the time and space to think about you. Women take longer to fall in love. Let her feelings for you grow. Avoid contacting her all the time early on. If she is more busy than you it's unattractive for her. Fill your life with fun, activity and abundance. Or at least behave that way. This is really attractive and the scarcity will make her want you more. Avoid being like every other guy hitting her up for dates. Instead, present her with the opportunity to chase you.

Summary of Attraction

In summary, there are four things that attract women and cause them to fall in love.

- Self Respect
- Internal strength
- Status
- Challenge

Her level of interest in you is directly related to how well you demonstrate these qualities. Anytime you demonstrate these qualities her interest goes up. Anytime you behave in an opposing way her interest goes down. The more attractive she is the more sensitive she will be to this. Focus on getting it right the majority of the time. Simple science but difficult to apply since most of it is counterintuitive to our learned behaviours.

Start to live upto these qualities and incorporate them into your life, actions and personality. Stay true to these values and she will eventually fall for you. That will take time because women fall in love much slower than men.

Now when she is in love with you, you can shift into relationship maintenance mode. Let's take a look at how to keep her in love with you.

Female Psychology In Relationships

Now if you lived up to the four attractive qualities and your girl is in love with you after around three months of dating. First of all, congratulations because most guys are rejected long before this stage. Incidentally many married women aren't even in love with their husbands.

The question now is, how do you keep her in love with you? This is a different scenario to attraction but it can still be broken down into four points. Most guys let themselves go at this point. They think the hard work is done so they can relax. They start taking their partner for granted. Work on your relationship and it will flourish. This will help you to avoid any surprise breakups, affairs or unhappy relationships. There are four specific things that will help keep your women in love with you.

Positivity

Keep your woman in love with you by giving her positivity. Most men fail miserably here. Once they get into a relationship they stop giving their woman positivity. Then they wonder why she is always unhappy.

The best way to give her positivity is to continue dating her. Even if you live a busy life make the time to go out on dates with her. Your goal should be to have a date night at least once a week. It doesn't need to be a big deal. Something simple like a coffee date, a trip to the movies or a walk in the park together is fine. It's all about purposeful and quality time together. Choose things to do together, on a specific time and date. If you really can't be bothered with it then maybe you should end the relationship and let some other guy take her out.

Another way to give her positivity is by giving her your full attention. Whenever she wants to show or tell you something, give her your full undivided attention. If it's at a busy moment for you then tell her you will be there in a little while. But when you do make sure it is with your full attention. Once you do that she will likely leave you to get on with whatever you were doing before. Make it a habit to give her positivity whenever she asks for it.

Whenever she does things that you like, let her know. This is positivity to her behaviour and it reinforces that positive dynamic in the relationship. Negative things are easy to notice but noticing positive things has a much more powerful result. Make it a conscious habit to focus on the positives of her. For example give her compliments:

"You look so sexy when you work out"

"Thanks for cooking me a delicious meal"
"You make me feel good"

In addition continue to say please, thank you, good morning and good night. All of these small things will stack up, put you in the best light and keep her in love with you. Actively create a positive relationship with her and she won't ever want to leave you.

Respect

When you are in a relationship with a woman give her respect. Never yell, shout at her or abuse her. There is never a good reason for you to lose your cool. If she really acts up, just walk away or calm down and deal with it appropriately later on. This is also about respecting yourself because the better you do that, the better you can respect your lover. She will appreciate and love you for this.

Make her feel comfortable to express herself in your relationship. This is achieved through respect. Respect her opinions and respect her for who she is. Let her talk about how she feels. Be there for her when she needs to express herself. Ask her if she needs your help. If she asks you for advice then give it to her. But if she doesn't, just listen. This is a rare and attractive trait.

Treat her like a strong and capable adult who is your equal. Have no double standards in your relationship. You might not always agree but everyone is different and you should respect them for who they are. It's a real sign of an alpha male. An alpha male who she will feel strongly in love with.

Humor

Life can be challenging for everyone at times. Good humour combined with a positive and fun attitude is one of the best ways to diffuse challenges and negativity in life. Never take yourself or your life too seriously. Don't worry be happy.

Have fun, entertain yourself and share it with your lover. Now that doesn't mean putting her down of having self-deprecating humor.
When things don't work out the way you expected, look for the funny side. For example:

- You booked a holiday and it didn't stop raining - stay inside and have great sex
- She fell over and got dirty - pick her up, laugh and kiss her
- You burned the dinner - laugh it off and order takeaway

Having a positive reframe of testing situations is very attractive. Most challenges are trivial so don't get all anal about them. Women love a man who is unfazed by challenges and obstacles. Maintain a light and fun, playful relationship dynamic with your woman. Your relationship will continue to flourish.

Teamwork

Teamwork makes the dream work! As cliche as it sounds, teamwork is one of the pillars to a long lasting and happy relationship. In a nutshell it means dating a woman who loves to do things for you without taking advantage of her and also doing things in return for her. We already have a mom so we don't need another one and plus we should be able to take care of ourselves by now. If your in a relationship with a woman who has a naturally giving personality make sure you reciprocate a little bit or at least give her appreciation. She will love you for it.

Try to be her equal in all things and share responsibilities. Map out the things that each of you will take care of. If she cooks, you clean. If she takes the kids to school, you pick them up. But make sure both of you agree on it being fair. This might seem trivial but by having that conversation and setting some simple boundaries it will allow your love to flourish.

Teamwork also includes giving her moral support, positive reinforcement and encouragement. When your out together, make her feel good to be with you. Consult with her about any big decisions in your life. Listen to her big decisions. Help each other out. Accept her for who she is and any imperfections or differences she has.

Summary of Female Psychology In Relationships

When a woman is in love with you completely make sure you fulfill the four requirements. Give her positivity, respect, humor and teamwork. This will keep her in love with you for as long as you want. It does take work but it's worth it to have a happy relationship full of love and good times.

If you feel that her love for you is fading then you need to roll back to demonstrating the four attractive male qualities. Then when her attraction for you is reignited you can start the relationship maintenance program again. Long term it is more of an advantage and easier to just use the relationship maintenance program than it is to keep building it up again and again. It's also more fulfilling to be in love with someone. That can run deep. Make sure you're actively creating something positive with the women in your life and you will be happy.

The Lover Provider Dichotomy

Understanding the lover provider dichotomy is another dynamic which will help you better understand female psychology. Consider it as an addition to what we have just discussed. In relationships men will typically go for women that they find to be physically attractive. Women on the other hand will usually separate men based on the attractive qualities discussed and also into two other categories. The lover and the provider.

Lover

This is the guy women are most sexually attractive to. Imagine a young model or a DJ who hooks up with lots of women. More than likely they are not quite financially stable enough to provide for a woman. The relationship is therefore mostly sexual. Women see lovers as men to hook up with.

If you want to fit into this category and bang lots of chicks then it's a good place to start. In that case get your looks on point. Ripped guys do well in this regard. When you meet women try to have sex with them as soon as possible.

I suggest you don't stay in this category for too long as the casual sex can start to become empty. Long term focus on improving yourself, going deeper and becoming more vulnerable. As a result, your relationships will improve.

Provider

This is the devoted husband who showers his wife in gifts and affection. A credible guy with a steady income who is willing to buy her stuff often. She gives him little sex and rarely finds him attractive. Long term the male must be dependable and able to provide for his children and partner.

From a biological standpoint women take a large risk in having sex with men. If they get pregnant then it needs to be with a provider type. Therefore women must be incredibly careful with their mating decisions regarding who they have casual sex with and who they marry.

Provider types are usually a beta male, not particularly attractive but very resourceful. They will often be made to wait for sex and later on rationed it. Eventually they will get laid after pursuing a woman for some time but otherwise they will get friendzoned. Once your in the friend zone getting out of it is pretty much impossible.

As an alpha male on the journey to becoming the best version of himself and attracting the best women the solution is to have a mix of both. Ravish her like a lover and be the confident provider type. Display the characteristics of the lover when you first meet a woman. Be a challenge, a bit of a bad boy with Status. She will be hot for you.

Hold back a little, don't show too much of your lifestyle. If she thinks your wealthy or a provider then she well make you wait longer. That will work against you. Seduce her. Then as you get to know her show her your lifestyle and that you can be a provider. Now that doesn't mean buying things for her. It's about being confident and outcome independent. Have your boundaries for what your willing to accept and not accept. If she is clearly a gold digger then move on.

You are an alpha male with a great life or are well on your way to a better life. Let's continue our journey.

Attractive Communication

The typical man to woman conversation goes something like this:

Man: "Hey what's your name?"
Woman: "Amy"
Man: "Where are you from?"
Woman: "Russia"
Man: "Oh nice I went there last year" "What do you do?"

The conversation usually quickly dries up and for both it is a pretty dull overall experience. Instead of asking questions make insightful statements. You can do this by first asking yourself the questions and then assuming their answers. Have an idea of the kind of woman you like other than her physical looks. Challenge her on these qualities.

Whenever you have a conversation with a woman there are three key things that you should think about which will instantly give you an insight into her mind and allow you to make powerful assumptions. I call it the PIE system. Anytime she gives you new information analyze her responses using the system.

For best results always ask open ended questions which will elicit more information. Open ended questions begin with: who, what, how, where, when and why? Go with the subjects that are likely to evoke emotions.

The skillset to achieve this kind of conversation relies on putting yourself in someone else's shoes. Being able to tell someone why you think they do something is a really powerful way of connecting with them.

Person:
What kind of person would do this? Adventurous, confident, romantic...

Inspiration:
What might she gain from doing this? New experience, passions, friends...

Emotion:
How would this make her feel? Happy, excited, alive...

Let's look at some examples of how this could work.

Example
You: "What do you like to do in your free time?"
Her: "I love shopping"
(person - trendy, inspiration - pass time, emotion - feel good)
You: "Wow, you are a real trendsetter! I can imagine the time must flyby when your shopping and feeling like a star trying on new clothes"
Her: "Yeah I love that feeling, do you think I would look good in Gucci?"

Example
You: "You look like your on vacation here"
Her: "Yeah it's my first time in Rome"
(person - adventurous, inspiration - new experiences, emotions - excitement)
You: "That's really adventurous! I can imagine you must get really excited to see new places"
Her: "Yeah this makes me feel alive, where are you from?"

Example
You: "What book are your reading now?"
Her: "It's a new romance novel"
(person - romantic, inspiration - entertainment, emotion - love)
You: "Those romance stories really capture your heart and feel the love. Tell you the truth, the best ones make you cry"
Her: "Oh my god yeah, have you ever been in love?"

Conversations like these will hook a girl right into you. You can instantly detect her interest level by the amount of talking she does and when she begins asking you more questions. This directly conveys her level of interest and commitment to the conversation. Ideally you should connect on things that are likely to have emotional attachment with them. These will help her to form closer bonds with you and make her feel like she has "known you for years." These include.

- **Travel:**

"If you could travel anywhere right now, where would you go?"
- **Childhood memories:**
"What were you like at school, the shy one, the leader?"
- **Passions:**
"What are you passionate about?"
- **Relationships:**
"Have you ever been in love?"
- **Food:**
"What food could you never give up?"

Indicator of Interest (IOI)

An indicator of interest is a verbal or non verbal sign of interest. IOIs can help you to know when a girl is into you or guage how interested she is.

Non-verbal IOIs:

- *She touches her hair*
- *Looks at you when you are in a group*
- *She stands close to you*
- *She touches you*
- *She is playful physically*
- *She brushes past you*
- *She holds your hand*

Verbal IOIs:

- *She asks you personal questions*
- *She asks about your female relationships*

- *She asks your name*
- *She asks what do you do*
- *She laughs at things you say*
- *She gives you compliments*
- *She sexualizes the conversations when you are talking*

Make the most of IOIs. If a girl gives you an IOI, don't hesitate to approach her. You can also force IOIs. For example, when you catch eyes with a woman, force her IOI by doing some kind of gesture. If it's funny she will respond and it's quite easy to open from there. Here are some examples of forcing IOIs.

- *Wave*
- *Make a funny face*
- *Smile*
- *Mirror her body language*
- *Blow a kiss*
- *Wink*

Push/Pull

As discussed earlier, Push/Pull is one of the most effective techniques to attract women. Women will become emotionally invested in you and chase you. Essentially push pull reverses the typical role of men chasing women and has them chasing you. This is achieved by giving them a rollercoaster ride of an interaction where you push and pull them. To further explain here are some examples:

Physical Push/Pull

Hug her and then say "alright, that's enough" and then softly push her away.

Pull her towards you, look into her eyes. Then sarcastically laugh as you shake your head and look away.

Give her a smile now and then and a frown now and then.

Emotional Push/Pull

"You have the cutest eyes I've seen today........No wait, actually the fourth best."

"Please go away, your way to hot and tempting."

"We would never get along, we are too similar."

Play with your own variations to make your interactions more interesting. It can also be used as a reward and punishment system where you reward her with pulls and punish her with pushes.

Tonality

Tonality is the oxygen of every conversation. The more tones that you are able to tap into, the more interesting you're going to be. Every time you're speaking your tonality is either getting people more invested or it is pushing them away.

There are three ways you can vary your tonality so you that command attention from the people listening to you.

All you need to remember is ASP:

- A = Amplitude
- S = Speed
- P = Pitch

If you can change your amplitude, speed or pitch every so often you will command infinitely more attention. Let's talk about the first one, amplitude. You can talk quietly and you can talk loudly. In nightclubs you should be talking loudly as a default to be heard over the background noise. Speed, every so often you can go a little bit faster and then slow things down for emphasis. Pitch you can talk in a very deep voice and at other times you can go higher.

Use ASP when you are talking with women. It will give more energy to your interactions and make you appear to be more charismatic.

Body Language

Great body language is a powerful way to communicate confidence and become attractive.

Stand tall with your chest lifted up and your shoulders back. Try not to hunch your shoulders. Suck in your stomach. If you work a lot on the computer always stretch out now and then to keep resetting your posture. Confident posture should become your new default.

Make sure your body language is symmetrical. Don't put more weight on one leg than the other. Symmetry is a powerful attractor. When you sit down, sit up straight and have your legs wide. Take up plenty of space.

Never cross your arms in front of your chest whilst talking. This sends signs that you are uncomfortable or closed off. If you have your hands in your pockets make sure they are in the back pockets or if in front ones with thumbs sticking out. Both of these positions will make you look more alpha. When you hold a drink, hold it loosely by your side. Not up in front of you. Overall you want to look confident, strong and relaxed.

Avoid leaning in when talking to a girl. It's almost always better to lean back because it communicates confidence and outcome independence. The only time you might want to lean in is to whisper something into her ear.

Maintain a relaxed and confident pace when you move. Calmly react to everything. Act like your the man and the world is yours. Slow head movements and long eye contact. Smile always, have a cocky look on your face. Carry yourself with pride and people will shower you with respect. At the start you can mirror or copy the body language of your favorite movie stars. Imagine how they would carry themselves.

Finally always make sure she is facing you. One of the keys of seduction is to not appear more interested in her. Her investment always need to be more. To make sure your conveying the best body language try filming yourself. Observe how you behave and if you have any unattractive behaviors or nervous ticks such as touching your face too much or fidgeting.

Kino

Kino is a pick up term used to descirbe the physical escalation from basic, intial touching to full sex. It is a powerful seduction method which begins when you first meet a woman and continues to build during the interaction. This can happen slowly or very quickly.

Begin with light touches when you first speak to a woman. This is completely non sexual such as a light touch on the arm. Women like to be touched because it conveys confidence. As she becomes more comfortable you can escalate the kino. Perhaps you hold her hand or touch her for longer periods of time. Ask about her jewelry, if she has tattoos, nails or read her palm. Use any excuse to touch her for longer. All of this builds comfort and familiarity towards physical intimacy.

Be confident and natural. Don't look at you hand when you touch her. If you sense she is uncomfortable, back off. If she is comfortable escalate. Two steps forward, one step back.

Sit closer to her, hold hands for longer, hug her, gaze into her eyes. As it starts to become a much more intimate interaction you should probably be somewhere appropriate. Massage her and suggest she take her top off. At this point you will naturally start kissing. Kissing leads to foreplay and then sex.

Remember at any signs of discomfort it's two steps forward, one step back. If your moves are rejected, relax and back up a couple of steps, then escalate again later on. If she doesn't comply, let it go and remember that you are outcome independent.

In some situations physical escalation can happen rapidly. Always ride that wave. The more experience you have the better you will become at reading the signs. I have met girls and had sex within minutes in a toilet without a word spoken. Sometimes you can jump steps!

To help you more check out some of my other books on confidence and communication.

Reading People: Harness the Power Of Personality, Body Language, Influence & Persuasion To Transform

Your Work, Relationships, Boost Your Confidence & Read People!

The Confident New You - Develop Your Confidence and Start Living The Life You Deserve

Where to Meet Women

Now that you know what women are attracted to, how to be an alpha male and how to talk with them your ready to start meeting women.

There are some key places you can meet women which we will discuss in the next chapters. Dating is a numbers game, the more women you come across the more your chances go up of having some kind of relationship with them. If your in a location that doesn't present enough women to you then make moves to be where you want to. Maybe that is a new city or even a new country. I had to do that and believe me it's totally worth it. Your luck will increase significantly.

The areas you can meet women all have there own negatives and positives but the key to all of them is to always be on. Life is a big game and you should talk to every girl you meet as if they are super hot. Make chit chat with people you come across in life. Practice makes perfect and this will put you at ease for when you actually meet attractive women. It will also make you great at socializing, have more confidence and always be on. Let's take a detailed look at some of the best places to meet women.

- **Night game**
  Meeting women at clubs, bars and so on.

- **Day game:**
  Meeting women in the daytime, malls, gyms and so on.
- **Online game:**
  Meeting women online, apps, websites and so on.
- **Social circle:**
  Meeting women through your social circle.
- **Jobs:**
  Meeting women through your work.

Each of the above will be discussed in detail over the following pages. Now let's go and meet some women!

Night Game

Around the world nightlife is pretty similar. Sexy girls in short skirts, make-up and high heels. People trying to look cool, high status and scanning the room. Loud music, drinking, dancing and having fun.

Successfully meeting and dating women at night requires mastery of a number of elements outlined in this chapter. It's important to note here that it will work best without the help of alcohol. Otherwise you will be building your skills on the requirement of you being tipsy or drunk. A few drinks when you are starting out is fine. Just don't build a habit out of it. That's fake confidence and will only hurt you in the long run. Gaming sober will feel awkward at first but with time you will grow into an alpha personality. Also it will help you with daygame. More on that later.

Before Going Out

Before you go out at night make some simple preparations.

Grooming:

Take a shower, brush your teeth, put on some cologne, style your hair and so on. Dress up in your best fitting and most fashionable clothes. You don't need a three piece suite. Just some cool jeans and a t-shirt that fits well. Feel good and good things will happen.

State:

The state you are in will dictate the results you achieve. State can be thought of as your general mood. When your working on a laptop all day you will be in a focused work state. This is antisocial and in that state your social skills aren't at their best. When your out and about you need to be in a good mood. So how do you transition from state to state?

Begin by relaxing yourself. Do some stretching, say some affirmations and things to put you in a good mood. Start to elevate yourself to a social state. Put on some music you love, dance and warm up your vocal cords by singing or humming. As soon as your out and about start talking with people and having fun. Make small talk with the taxi driver, open people on the way to the club and get in a social mood as quickly as possible.

Get a good wing

If you have people to go out with that will dramatically increase your results. They can help you open groups, pump up your state and push you through hard times. They can be girls or guys. Always be making friends including in the venue that night where you can find some wings. Build some rapport and then go hit it up.

Don't be put off if you have to go out solo. Just be social and have a good time.

Venues

There are four different types of venues that you can visit at night. Get to know the most popular in your area and what nights are the best to visit each on. Fill your week up with events and places to go. Let's take a look at the different types of venues.

Bars

Popular bars attract lots of fun loving people. The environment is social and it's easy to bounce around talking to different people. Older and more intellectual crowds frequent bars so conversations will be more in depth with less physical dancefloor game.

Lounges

These are similar to bars but will be more quiet and attract different types of people. They include, hotel bars, shisha bars and cocktail lounges. Normally people don't come here to party but instead they come for an event or just to relax. Here you will meet more upmarket clientele so dress to impress. In addition solo female travelers, older women and business women are often found here unwinding. The best time to go would be early on in the evening.

Nightclubs

Nightclubs are the most popular night time venues. They have a dancefloor, bar, DJ and lots of entertainment. Younger crowds and hot girls can be found at these. Nightclubs are a great place to dive into learning game since you will meet many women there, most nights of the week. You can also take advantage of all the scenarios in a nightclub such as pulling girls to the dancefloor or for drinks at the bar. The connections you make in nightclubs will be more superficial and likely to result in one night stands at the most. Although you can also meet girlfriend material types here.

Events

Events, festivals and meetups at night are great places to meet lots of women. Often these are frequented by busy, interesting women who don't have the time to waste in bars and clubs. Go there to have fun and talk with lots of women. Keep upto date with the best events in your area.

When to go out

When your first learning game you should go out every night of the week or as much as possible. Even if that's just for a few hours because it will desensitize you and help you to improve rapidly. If you can spread that across a few different venues then that's great. Ideally you want to move to a city that has a bunch of different nights on each week. For example, ladies nights on Sundays, hip hop on Thursdays and so on. As you become more advanced you can go out less. However make sure you never stop going out!

How much time you spend when your out is also important. At the start you should spend at least three hours out. Set your timeframes and don't compromise. If you have to be up early the next day then don't stay out past a certain time. Regardless if the girl is down, you are the man and you set the standard. Have boundaries.

The best time to go out will vary from each place so become aware of the peak times. Girls will often become more social later on into the night. The first part of the night should involved kicking back and enjoying the place. Pulling comes much later on.

Social Proof

Social proof is highly attractive to women, especially in night time venues. Women rely on social proof from the environment to identify if you are a cool, alpha man or not. This is processed by her on a conscious and subconscious level.

This is the reason why you should have fun and talk to lots of people when your out. Not only will it put you into a great mind state it will also raise your social value in the venue. DJ's and club management get laid a lot because of this. They have massive social proof.

Compliment other guys, cheers with people and be friendly. At the start focus on building social proof. With this grounding girls are likely to come hit on you and also opening them will be easy. When people see that you are the life and soul of the party it adds a ton of social value to you.

Enjoy the music and have fun. Regardless of whether you get laid that night or not your number one priority should be to have fun. Remember one of the most attractive characters of a man is outcome independence.

This is all about getting out of your head and into the moment. Don't just stand there scanning the room. Instead cheers people, smile, say hi and be social. Build positive social momentum and acquire social proof.

Identifying the women to approach

Identifying the women to approach will save you a lot of hassle and time. The skill that relies on analyzing social cues and signals from women. On a general level there are certain things you can pay attention to, from the obvious to the not so obvious. For example.

- Avoid girls on tables full of guys
- Avoid girls who are clearly wasted

- Avoid girls who talk to every single guy

That should be enough to get you going because you don't want to limit your options too much. Sometimes a girl might look standoffish and unapproachable but in fact many times I have approached these kind of girls and they have turned out to be lovely. If you get rejected don't let that get to you. Just look for the funny side of it, congratulate yourself for having the balls to do it and then move swiftly on.

Opening

When you first see a woman you like in a club there are a few ways you can guarantee your future success with them. First of all your going to need to open her, unless she open's you first. There are a number of ways you can open a woman in a nightclub. Here are some examples.

Indicator of Interest (IOI):

Girls give off clues that they are into you. That could include smiling at you, making lots of eye contact or touching you. You can also force her IOI by gesturing at her from waving to sticking your tongue out. Make sure you respond to her IOI in a fun way. Then you can easily open her. Always be smiling and projecting confidence.

Low Pressure Openers

Low pressure openers are easy to pull of but have a low yield of success. If your feeling a bit stifled do a couple of these. Rejection is unlikely and you can just say them then walk off. She will be easy to open again later on and talk more with.

- *Cheers glasses with her*
- *Say: "Nice to meet you"*

Energy Openers

This kind of opener works well in nightclubs and with groups because it involves boosting the energy of the people you open. Simply just come in with an energetic:

"Hey, are you having fun!" or

"Whats Up!"

Make sure you calibrate well with this. Only use it on people who are having a good time. Not people chilling out.

This works the best on the dancefloor where there is a lot of energy. You can go in with a non verbal opener. My favorite thing to do is to make a brief IOI with a girl then spin her salsa style. Right away you will be dancing with her, which is very intimate. If you do this, try to get some basic dance moves locked down. Take up a few salsa classes, you will also meet women at them.

Observational Openers

These openers are pretty effective, just make a statement about the environment. The more fun these are the better the girl will respond. For example:

"Cool dress, but maybe it would look better on me"
"It's like a sausage party in here tonight!"
"Oh my god, look at that girls butt...it's huge!"

Direct Openers

These openers involve going up to a girl and stating your direct interest in her. Say them with confidence and charisma to improve your chances. For example:

"Hi you look great tonight, I'm Darcy nice to meet you"
"Hey, you have an amazing body by the way, nice to meet you, I'm Darcy"

Make sure you have already got some social proof in the venue and are well calibrated in your approach. For example these probably won't work so well if you interrupt her whilst she is dancing or with her friends.

Group Openers

If you see a girl in a group that you like don't let that put you off approaching her. There are a couple of ways you can pull this off. First of all, make sure you have established some basic IOI with her. Then you can open her with a simple intro at the side of the group. Just make sure that later on you have the approval of her friends otherwise they might block your chances. This can be achieved by having her introduce you to them.

The other way to open a girl in a group is to do it through one of her friends. Look for the leader of the group, maybe her gay best friend and so on. Approach them, introduce yourself, maybe buy them a drink and then build some basic rapport. Ask about the girl and then have them introduce you. Again with this kind of approach timing and calibration is everything. Make sure to only approach a group that looks open and is having a good time. Not one that has just arrived or is closed off in the VIP area.

If you get rejected move on swiftly to the next set and keep having a good time. At least you approached!

In set

The first conversations you have with girls in clubs should be fun and exciting. Deep conversations won't go down well in loud clubs full of drunk people. Save those for the pillow talk. Cover a range of topics, tell stories, make fun of her and talk about the environment. Be extraverted, ridiculous and fun. Have a go to of stories that you regularly use. These should convey high value and fun. For example.

- That time a crazy chick tried to pull you to the bathroom
- The music being played
- How her hair is styled

Stay talking to her for as long as possible. Even if the conversation dips just become comfortable with the awkwardness or silences. No trying to fill them with nonsense. If it is really dry or your not into the girl make your excuses and leave. Otherwise take the time to build some rapport using the attractive communication methods to make assumptions and connect with her.

Now you don't need to stick to her the whole night. Come back now and then as you enjoy the night. At the start you should get her contact information incase you can't find her later.

There will probably be some awkward moments during the night such as other guys coming in or interference from her friends. Just be non reactive and stay cool.

Investment

All the time you should be focused on getting the girl more invested into you. There are a number of ways you can achieve this and they should be stablemates to your night game.

Challenge

Remember you are the buyer and you are screening her. Challenge her by asking her questions that put you into that frame. For example:

- *"Why are you here tonight?"*
- *"What else do you have besides your looks?"*

Keep coming up with these things in you mind whilst your talking to her. Always be thinking, "I'm such a bad ass and she is so lucky."

Move

Moving a girl around the venue will get her invested in you and make it much easier to lead her out of the venue later on. Take her to the dancefloor. Take her to the bar and so on. You don't need to stick to her all night. Take breaks here and there. Be confident in yourself.

Have her introduce you to her friends. Again this gets here more invested into you. In addition it reduces the chances of her friends interfering with your interaction. In fact if they like you they will be likely to push her to you. Charm them.

Pull

Towards the end of the night you need to think about how to take the girl home.

Seed

Keep planting seeds in her mind about coming home with you. Say subtle things like "I'm gonna kidnap you" or "maybe we can go somewhere private later". Start planting seeds in her mind right from when you first meet.

Logistics

During your interaction there are three important things you need to figure out. These will let you know whether you should pursue pulling her that night, get a number or abort the mission.

- Who is she here with?
- Where does she live?
- What is she doing tomorrow?

Lead

If she has good logistics, you have built enough attraction, have isolated her and spent quality time with her then you can first suggest to go outside and get some fresh air. Don't rush into this unless she is really down. She should already be compliant and in your frame, moving wherever you want her to. Having her take that step outside of the club makes it very easy to transition into taking her home.

Once she is outside I usually just hail a cab. If she asks where we are going to just say "afterparty" or "I have a music studio" or something fun. In the taxi or during the walk keep her logical mind distracted. Keep pumping the fun and happy vibes. Keep doing kino as well.

If she came as part of a group it will help you massively if you are polite and fun with her group. Then they will help you to pull her and not object to you taking her home. In addition your perception of being high status will help. Otherwise you can do bathroom pulls and stuff like that if it is a venue where you can pull that off. But preferably you should take her home.

If you can't pull, build rapport, take the number and arrange a date later using the texting system.

Taking Her Home

When you reach your place don't jump straight on her (unless she is really horny and you have been making out in the taxi, etc). Set the mood and tone of the room. Put on some dim lights, background music and make some drinks. You can then show her some pictures or videos and then start to escalate physically. More on that in the sex chapter.

If you go to her place, again remain cool and don't jump straight on her, unless she is really down. Only go to her place if it is more convenient or she suggests it.

The Challenge

Here are some challenges to get you started. Diary your progress and let me know at
www.darcycarter.com

- Go out and cheers with ten people
- Go out and open five girls and two guys
- Go out and get the number of two girls
- Go out and pull a girl home for sex

Day Game

Day game is the art of approaching and talking to women in real day to day life. No bars, clubs, online or social circle. Parks, coffee shops, the gym, shopping malls, train stations and so on. Incorporate this into your life. Flirt with the supermarket cashiers, people you come across and so on. Ideally do that away from where you live because at the start you will come off as uncalibrated and weird. If you have the luxury, then travel to the next city.

Learning day game takes a while because there is a lot of social pressure involved in it. Particularly more so in some places more than others. For example in some countries eye contact and smiling at strangers is weird. Whilst in others it is standard procedure. Regardless don't let any social conditioning affect you. If you calibrate yourself well, and approach with confidence none of that will matter. You will meet all kinds of women in day time.

Focus on having great eye contact and vibes. Smile and be warm.

Incidentally, you should always be smiling when your out daygaming. It will put you into a good mood and attract positive emotions to you. I usually have a cheeky half smile most of the time. When people catch eyes with me they often get a nice happy shock because most people are walking around in a zombie state. In addition, make sure your body language is confident. Chest out, stomach in and shoulders back.

There are five key components of success in daygame.

Open

As you might of guessed this is the part where for the first time you talk to a new woman. There are two ways you can do this. Note that before you use any of the two ways you should first get her attention with a "hello" or "excuse me". Otherwise she will be unlikely to hear your opener. Also before you open her smile. Say excuse me, pause and smile. Then you can go into your opener.

Indirect

This is a low pressure opener since your not showing her any personal interest. When your starting out this is helpful. However indirect openers are not particularly useful if you want to actually close a girl since it can be quite difficult to transition into something personal. However if your struggling or starting use an indirect. Examples:

- Ask her for directions
- Ask her for the time

Direct

Direct openers are where you actually state your interest in a girl. These require more confidence but the results can be powerful. Men rarely do this and most girls will find it to be charming. Before going direct it's a good idea to get her compliant. For example:

- *"Excuse me, do you speak english?"*
- *"Excuse me, are you from around here?"*

The above statements serve two purposes. One, they get her to say yes to you and to be compliant. Two, it gauges whether or not you should continue or leave. For example, if she doesn't speak english then you would be wasting your time. Unless you speak her language or exchange numbers on a translation app such as Wechat. Incidentally I have actually pulled many girls who didn't speak my language using this method. Google translate and Wechat can be wonderful for the dating life!

After your compliance statements you can move to your direct opener. For example:

"I noticed you look really smart and wanted to say hi"
"I saw you and you look really cute, so I wanted to introduce myself"
"You look beautiful and I couldn't resist saying hi"

Assumptions

When you first open a girl in the daytime and in fact anytime try not to ask too many questions. Questions at the start either put too much pressure on her and/or are boring. Put in all the work at the start and get her hooked on to you. Make assumptions to get her talking. These come after a pause after the opener. After making an assumption pause and give her time to respond. This will make you look calm and confident.

With assumptions, the more playful and fun they are the better. Try not to go over the top with these though since the day game requires a bit more conservative behaviour. Save the extraversion for night game. Let's take a look at some examples and threads you can use.

    A. Where is she from

"I was thinking that you look very formal and polite, I guess your British."

"I was thinking, you look very glamorous you must be from New York"

    B. What she does for a job

"You know you look really smart you must be a very successful person"

"You look like your in great shape I guess your a yoga instructor or coach"

C. What she is doing right now

"I noticed you standing there and I was thinking this girl is either waiting for a date or some cool guy to come say hi"

"You look really healthy, you must be off to the gym right now"

Give her time to respond to your assumptions. You can also keep stacking them as go, gauge her responses and then calibrate accordingly. Practice this skill by observing people throughout the day. Concote stories about them in your mind.

Rapport

Rapport is when you start to move forward in the interaction. Go along with one of the threads that she responded well to from your assumptions. This is when you can start to build connections. During this stage you want to tease her and be playful. Avoid the Mr nice guy chit chat here. None of that "where are you from?" and "What do you do?" stuff.

When she gives you a topic drill it, tease on it, show mutual interest and move to a close. Let's take a look at some potential scenarios.

Example A

You: "I noticed you standing there and I was thinking this girl is either waiting for a date or some cool guy to come say hi"
Her: "Haha actually I'm waiting for my friend"
You: "Ahh that's a relief then, there is no jealous boyfriend on the way. I can't believe a girl like you would be single. You must be married"
Her: "Wow thanks, actually I'm just dating at the moment"
You: "Awesome, then today is my lucky day. Wait unless you're one of those crazy people?"

Notice in this example I was able to find out if she is single or not which saves lots of time. Then I am also challenging her but in a playful way that builds attraction.

Example B

You: "I was thinking that you look very formal and polite, I guess your British."
Her: "No, I am Russian"
You: "Ahh yes now I see the high cheekbones and elegance. Let me guess your out here on a date or maybe your working as an international spy"
Her: "You are a funny man. What do you want?"
You: "I'm interested to know you more and would like to suggest we grab some coffee".

Notice in this example the girl is a little bit standoffish. However she shows some signs of interest and is being particularly direct. In this situation being more direct will help dramatically to either move forward or save time and leave.

Example C

You: "You look really healthy, you must be off to the gym right now"
Her: "Haha thanks, actually I am going to teach yoga now"
You: "Great I can tell, you look fit and seem really calm. Anyway you must be in a rush. It would be great to talk with you more, do you have any applications to stay in contact?"
Her: "Thanks, but sorry I have a boyfriend"
You: "No worries have a great day"

Notice in this example the interaction moved quickly. This is because it's obvious she was in a rush. Although it ended without any number that's fine because these things happen. Move on to the next.

During this stage as she elicits more information you can begin to build more rapport with open ended questions. These are questions that evoke more than one word answers. Such as:

"What's your favorite thing about this town"?
"What brings you here"

Try to keep things situational and also relatable. This will make it easier to transition into closing. You can also restate her answers back to her in an emotional way. Kind of like assumptions again and again. Make sure you also tell her about yourself so you don't come across as just some guy she met on the street. Relate to her on the subjects. For example:

Her: "I'm a certified yoga instructor"
You: "Awesome, I love practicing yoga in the mornings. It makes me feel happy and relaxed"

Her: "I'm here on a business trip"
You: "That's great you can travel and work, we share that. I love having the freedom to be wherever I want."

Close

Every interaction should have an end goal. That goal is either a date, lay or relationship. The quicker you can get to those, the better. More often than not day game interactions end in a number close. Where you say something like:

"It's been great talking to you. How can we stay in touch?"

Let her decide on what contact information she prefers to give you. The best is usually an app such as Wechat or instagram which will keep you updated on each others lives and allow you to chat.

Alternatively you can go on a date there and then. This is the ideal situation because it's fresh in her mind. Simply suggest you go have coffee nearby or sit nearby. In some situations you might even get laid in the day time. I have, and reading signs of interest from a girl is critical to achieving this.

Approach Anxiety

When you first start day game you will likely be riddled with approach anxiety. Everyone has felt it, you see that gorgeous girl and you feel a strong desire to talk to her, but you don't. The feeling can be overwhelming and cloud your judgement.

The best way to overcome this is to immerse yourself in it. In fact approach anxiety will affect you in night game and day game. It's when you feel too nervous to approach a girl. This never goes away but there are ways to deal with it.

For a lot of guys it comes from low self esteem and low confidence issues. These need to be resolved first. Fix your inner game and prime your state. Defeat those negative thoughts. Think about it like this. Women want to meet cool guys and if your a fun, normal guy than you are at the top of the pack. Stop putting women up on a pedestal and realize that they are just a person with their own flaws.

Realize that it's better to have some short term suffering of social pressure but long term you benefit from it. She could be in your bed. And if she rejects you then it's better than rejecting yourself and regretting it all day. Just go up and find out. There really is nothing to fear, the worst that could happen is she tells you to get lost. Then at least you saved yourself time by not linking up with a rude girl. In any case that rejection is not personal, she could just be having a bad day. There are a billion reasons as to why she might turn you down.

Fear of rejection is worse than the rejection itself. Let go of any outcomes. That just puts unnecessary pressure on you. The only thing you should have the goal to do is to simply go up and say "hi". As you become more comfortable then you can push things further. If she rejects you or acts rude don't let it affect you. Move on. You will walk away feeling like a champion regardless. Keep working at your approaches everyday.

The Challenge

Here are some challenges to get you started. Diary your progress and let me know at
www.darcycarter.com

Easy:
For the next ten days open 5 people everyday. That can be a simple hi.
Reach 50 then move to medium challenge.

Medium:
Get five numbers from day game in ten days. It does not matter if they respond. Just get a number.

Advanced:
Get a date or a lay from daygame.

Job Game

Going out day and night meeting women can be tiring, time consuming and often fruitless. Imagine a job where you get paid and get laid! We spend most of our lives earning an income. Wouldn't it be great to kill two birds with one stone? After all life is a game and you should always be on meeting women. Incidentally I am a DJ and believe me this has got me laid countless times from super hot women!

Here are some of the best jobs to meet new women.

DJ or Musician

Being a DJ or musician is going to put you into social situations and give you high status. Many people regard them as having power in the club or venue. Women find this highly attractive. Opening will be much easier, just go up and introduce yourself.

Personal Trainer

The majority of people who use personal trainers are women. In most cases they are pretty hot women with great bodies. Working out at the gym with someone naturally involves kino and intimacy. Closing a girl from the gym becomes much easier when your an authority there who has already established physical intimacy. You also have unlimited low risk approach options. Need some help with that squat?

Tour guide or instructor

Anyone working in tourism or adventure activities is going to have a stream of girls constantly coming to them. Girls often travel with other girls or even alone. If your working in this industry, you get to spend a long period of time alone with them. Incorporate the alpha traits and you will have them chasing you.

Photographer

Chicks love to be photographed. It's so easy to get started. Buy yourself a decent camera, learn the skills online and then start offering free shoots to girls. Find a decent place to take pictures. Make them comfortable and behave as a true alpha. If your taking lingerie and nude shots then closing becomes very natural since the girl will likely be turned on. This works best with amateur photography. Professional models will of course act more professionally. But you can still date them and likely close later on.

Bartender or club staff

Every night these guys have access to tons of girls. They also have tons of social proof where they work. All you have to do is be charismatic and confident. Closing will be easy, you can take their number or just wait until closing time and take them home.

Massage therapist

What girl doesn't love a good sensual massage? Women love a guy who is good with his hands. If you look decent and have some great game then you can easily close any hotties that come your way. When your dating girls bring this up and it gives you an excuse to bring them home.

Tattoo artist

This one has the stigma of being a bad boy and artist. Both are super attractive to women. They will also be half naked or more when you have to tattoo them which leads to more intimacy. Having a tattoo is a very emotional experience and women will relate that to you. Tattoo artists often date multiple women at a time.

Model agent or PR

Believe me there guys have huge databases of the hottest women. Plus they usually have access to exclusive venues, tables and so on. Women will literally fall at their feet to get into their world. You won't really need much game with this kind of role since the social status and value is already so high.

Student

Technically not a job. But if your a dude spending most of your days on campus then realize your sitting on a gold mine. Women love to study. Take up some classes and meet more women.

Office Job

Office jobs are going to be difficult to get laid in and probably create an uncomfortable situation for you. It's a long process, has limited options and high risks. Better to try one of the above, even if it's just part time.

Whatever job you are in, make the most of it. Present your best self at all times and always be on. Ready to meet new women.

Social Circle Game

Social circle game is all about building a social network that introduces you to endless women. Think about your current social circle. It's well known that the people we hang around with shape us. Try and cut out the people who don't know many people or are dead ends. Aim to hang out more with people who are well connected. People such as PR managers, agency owners, DJ's and so on. Get to know the staff of the clubs you go to. From the door man to the PR to the manager. They will get you quick access, entry to exclusive parties and connections.

Make a habit of becoming more interested in other people.

When you take an interest in other people it makes you more likeable. That doesn't mean just the hot girls. Everyone has friends and some of them will be connected to hot women. Aim to build a network of really cool people to hang out with regularly. They can invite you to exclusive parties, get you into vip sections and introduce to gorgeous women.

It's important to note here that not every women you talk to should be thought of as having sex with or not. Making friends with women is a great idea if you want to meet even more of them. I often friendzone really hot women for that reason.

Add value to the people that you hang out with. Invite them to the activities that your involved in. Otherwise you can bring people to the events that your PR friends might be hosting. Then your bringing them social proof and more connections.

Start off in your local area

Familiarize yourself with the local shop, the places you like to eat at, coffee shops, library and so on. Be friendly, polite and tip them. This sets up an abundance mentality and sources of positivity. When you take a girl out to one of those places it will give you social proof since people hold you in high regard there. In addition if your there alone and a cute girl enters it will be much easier and comfortable for you to approach her.

Finally it will help you to be in a positive state most of the time since your engaging with people throughout the day. Always make the effort to ask people in these places and how they are. Say hi and wish them a great day.

Keep working on your social skills because how you do one thing is how you do everything. Aim to communicate with at least three people a day. People will find it refersing that someone actually took the time to say hi and show them some interest.

Get involved in the local community and build an active social life. Spend as little time at home as possible. Check out www.meetup.com for some activities to get involved in. Try some classes and sports for finding more friends. Find out about events going on in your local area. This could be festivals, celebrations, concerts and so on. There will be lots of local people here that you can make friends with or date. Get out of the house, the only time you should be there is when you are sleeping. Look for opportunities to be social.

Inevitably with this kind of purpose you will build a social circle of like minded individuals. Ideally you should have at least four to five people in your close circle. This is great because you will always have people to go out with and help you with talking to girls. I often have one of my girls go over to a group of girls to open them for me since it is less threatening to them and adds massive social value to me.

Good times.

Online Game

The online dating scene is overloaded with desperate guys looking for a woman. Not only that but the ratio of men to women is on average six to one. There are some hungry and desperate guys there!

Standing out from the crowd will require you to be different. Show women that you are the one who is selecting and she needs to win you over. That should be your mindset. Remember the list of qualities you look for in a woman? Use this when your talking to girls online to screen them for those qualities.

Keep her off the pedestal. The biggest mistake guys make online is projecting their ideals onto a woman. Just because she is hot and likes reading doesn't make her a goddess. Many guys will straight away declare their interest and describe how they would be perfect for each other. This comes across as creepy and needy. Convey your confidence and outcome independence throughout.

There are a number of apps and sites you can use to meet women. We are now in an amazing time where it is really easy to meet women. You can literally come into contact with women on the other side of the world. Which is great if your planning to go there next week. Anyway, let's take a look at some of the best dating applications and websites.

Tinder

Tinder is the big daddy of dating apps with most users. It's a well known fact that there are way more men on Tinder than women. Not only that but women are way more selective on Tinder than men and match up to twenty times more than them. To stand out your going to have to optimize your profile and have a great strategy.

Photos

If you want success on Tinder than you need great photos or videos. Six photos should be more than enough. Consider the following.

Profile photo

Your profile picture is the number one biggest selling tool that you have on Tinder. First impressions mean everything here and women will swipe mostly depending on your profile picture. Pay attention to your main profile picture.

The first and most important rule when identifying which profile picture to use is to make sure it was taken within the past twelve months. If you meet up and they see you look much older or different from your picture then it will be pretty much over at that point because you lied and misrepresented yourself.

Avoid:
- Selfies, low quality photos, old pictures, out of focus or obscured by sunglasses, hats and so on.

Use:
- A high quality image of you alone showing the upper half of your body. If your looking away from the camera and smiling that works well. Make sure your well dressed and looking your best. If you have a cat or animal in the picture that can work well also. It should be a candid shot. No glamorous shots or posed shots.

Other photos

Okay so you have a great profile picture now let's talk about the other pictures. Six pictures will be more than enough. Don't be one of these people that has twenty pictures or more because that only increases the chances of someone finding something they don't like about you. So let's now talk about the additional pictures.

If you don't have these extra perfect pictures get a friend or hire someone and spend the day taking these pictures. This is going to improve your internet dating experience tenfold.

Photo Two, Group Shot:

Having a group photo shows that you are a likeable guy with a good set of family and friends. Women don't want to date dangerous reclusive guys. Group shots show her that your normal, gives you social proof and makes her want to get to know you.

Make sure that the photo is authentic, candid and not posed. For example it could be of you and your friends on holiday or doing something fun in the moment.

Photo Three, Body Shot:

This is not going to be some shirtless bathroom selfie but instead something that shows her that your in good shape from head to toe. This again should also be candid and not posed. It's best if it tells some kind of story such as you at the gym or your taking boxing classes for example. Photos should always tell a story and show your attractive traits.

Photo Four, High Status:

Girls love guys with high status. You don't need to loaded and dripping with gold. Just convey that you are a man of quality. A simple picture with a suit on is more than enough. Or it could be you giving a presentation and so on. You might work as a mechanic but you still need a picture that is you all dressed up.

Photo Five, Adventure:

Adventure and travel are really attractive to women. You can convey this through your photos with some location shots at tourist destinations. Or you can put some pictures up of you doing cool and adventurous activities such as skydiving, skiing and so on. These kinds of photos will give her something to connect with you on.

Photo Six, Lifestyle:

Finally give her a little more insight into your life to verify that your cool and a grounded alpha male. This could be something simple like you in nature with friends, reading books or whatever it is you like to do. Or it could be a casual picture of you with friends. Even better if they are attractive women. Just make sure it looks great.

Writing Your Bio

A well written bio is going to put you closer to the top of the stack. But what should you write in your bio? Here are some things to help you.

Headline

Your bio headline will make or break the first impression of you. The headline needs to be simple, concise and fun. Three to four sentences is more than enough. Anymore and she probably won't read it.

Show don't tell

Instead of saying I'm this or that actually give examples. These don't have to be completely true, humor works wonders here.

Alpha male = "I once wrestled a bear"

Adventurous = "Travelled to forty two countries, any suggestions for where I should go next?"

Attractive = "Catch me every week DJing in the best clubs"

Be risky

Avoid sounding boring, it's better to push the boundaries when describing yourself.

Businessman = "I took the red pill and escaped the matrix"

Enjoy long walks = "I enjoy long walks but hopefully your not one of those annoying people, otherwise I might push you off the cliff."

Recently single = "My last ex threw a brick through my window."

Foodie = "Bake me a cookie and you might get lucky"

Add in emojis and stats

Your profile should be quick to read. Emojis and stats will help here. If your from a particular country or living somewhere use the flag emoji. If your tall, list your height. If you like music use the music emoji and so on.

Swiping Strategy

Once and only once your profile is set up should you start swiping. If you don't get many matches then tweak your pictures and bio description. The better your profile is the more you will appear in front of women. Paying for Tinder will also help, more on that later. Some other things that will help your chances are:

Being selective

If you swipe right on every single profile this communicates to Tinder that your low value and should therefore be at the bottom of the pile. Be selective in your swiping. Only swipe the women that you really find attractive. Then make sure you message everyone you match with.

Send quality messages and Tinder will give you preference since women are going to be more responsive to you. The algorithm is skewed in advantage of women on Tinder so you need to be perceived as being more attractive. This is easy work if you have a great profile and an awesome strategy.

Superlikes

Whenever you super like someone that gives them a notification and raises you to the top of their swiping stack. In essence it increases your chances of being seen by them. Use it if you really want to get noticed by someone. However it is not guaranteed that you will match with them.

Opening Message

Once you have successfully matched with a girl you can start talking with her. Your opening message will set the tone of the conversation. Make the opener fun and encouraging for her to reply to. Avoid any cliche lines that are clearly hitting on her.

The first message is a lot simpler than you might think. Most guys get confused here, thinking they need to send some amazing first message. Really, it's not that complicated. But to maximize your results stick to a framework.

- *Scan through her profile*
  Look for things that you can spin off. This shows her that you took the time to read her profile (which most guys don't). Make a comment on her love of dancing, or where she has travelled to and so on.

- *Compel her to respond*
  You can do this by ending your message with a simple open ended question such as.
  "Interesting profile picture, where was it taken?" or "love the jeans in picture 3, where can I buy them?"
- *Keep the first message short*
  A few sentences will be more than enough. Don't write an essay.
- *Gif*
  Tinder has some cool gifs you can send. These have a high response rate and can be sent quickly on mass.

Communication

The best communication strategy on Tinder is to be authentic and fun. Start connecting with her on various subjects and throw in some challenges with rapport breaks here and there. Make assumptions, build connections and utilize the texting strategy from this book.

Closing

Once she seems into you and you have built some commonalities, get her number or contact information for another application. Transitioning to another application raises her investment in you and allows you to set up a date with ease. Say something like the following.

"You seem cool. Drop me your number and we can chat a bit more☺"

Alternatively you can set up a date on Tinder or even invite her over to your place directly.* Make sure she is congruent and down for it. Test her responses to risky conversation. You can always pull back if she seems put off by it. For example:

"Cute butt" or "Gonna take a hot shower now"

* This could lead to a more sexual conversation. If she is negative towards it hold the frame and quickly move onto safer topics. For example, she might say something like "ew creep". In that case just disregard it by saying "lol, just kidding" then move on. Otherwise lead to more sexual topics and have her over to your place.

Meeting up with women online

Once you've bantered and are ready to ask her out on a date, you can proceed to asking her out. Make sure your leading towards a date of some kind of meeting. In some situations it would be appropriate to invite her directly to your house. Only do that if your established enough attraction and have a good vibe going on. Otherwise you can start finding out her availability and then suggest some date ideas. More on that later.

Tinder Gold

Tinder Gold is a premium paid service. You can get it cheaper if your under thirty years old. If your over that age then just create a new Facebook profile with an age under thirty and use that to log in. Tinder Gold offers the following.

- Unlimited Likes = never run out again.
- Rewind last swipe = if you accidentally swiped past that hottie, bring her back!
- Five super likes per day = you get noticed more.
- One boost each month = raises you to the top of the stack for thirty minutes and gets you lots of matches
- Passport = allows you to swipe anywhere in the world regardless of your current location. This is great for setting up dates somewhere you're planning to visit. Do this at peak user time between 8pm and 10pm.
- See who likes you = as it says.

Other Dating Sites and Applications

There are hundreds of other online dating applications and websites where you can start talking to women nearby right away. Try out some of the best and go with what works for you, wherever you happen to be located in the world.

Instagram

Right now Instagram is one of the hottest apps for meeting women. Done correctly it can put you into contact with an abundance of women, give you social proof and improve your dating life.

To start, search for the most popular places in your area. Locations such as shopping malls, clubs, bars, gyms, tourist hot spots and so on. Search for the location and a bunch of photos posted by people there will show up. You could even search some locations your planning to visit. Then you can scroll through until you find some hot chicks.

The process is a numbers game so hit up as many women as possible. The best strategy I have found is as follows.

- Like a bunch of her pictures.
- Wait a few days to see if she reciprocates

- If she does, follow her. Then if she follows you back send her a DM.
- Then you can use the text game strategy outlined in this book.

Dating success tends to work best on girls with under twenty thousand followers. Girls with more than that are less likely to respond because you will be lost in the sea of likes spam. But if you insist, just send her a DM. An emoji should be fine. You might get a response. I have before with girls having over 100k followers.

Now it's important to note that all of the above does rely on your Instagram profile being optimized. If you have a lame profile with lame pictures then you won't get any results. Your profile should spark her interest. Do something similar to what you would for your Tinder profile.

- Have a good profile picture
- Have an engaging bio
- Post cool pictures that are high quality, high status, fun and engaging

The first message you send can be indirect or direct.

Examples:

"Hey! I will be visiting your city next week, any cool places I should check out?"

"Great pictures!"
Comment on something from her pictures or bio.

Then make sure you screen them to find out if they have a boyfriend, how long they are here for and so on.

Facebook

Facebook is another great way to meet women online. This relies more on the number of friends you have since Facebook will only suggest people you might know based off of your current friends list. Add girls who look cool and attractive. If they add you back you can then start messaging each other.

Open with something simple such as.

"Nice to meet you"

Or comment on something about her profile. Or how you two are connected. From there on you can use the text game strategy and screening to check her availability.

Again make sure your profile is up to date with good pictures and quality posts. Don't want fill your wall up with stupid stuff from games or political things and so on. Girls will take all of this into account before they add you. Having photos of you being social, having fun and even with other girls will help massively. Follow the Tinder guide for more ideas.

Adding girls on social media will require building a lot of comfort and investment before they are willing to meet you. Make sure you keep pumping her attraction and engagement as well with regular posting and so on.

After you have been chatting with her for a while you can suggest a meet. If she seems genuinely interested then make this happen as soon as possible. You can gauge her interest by how much she replies and the depth of her replies. If she is texting back and forth with you and asking questions then she is likely into you. If she takes days to reply and is very low interest then forget her and move on.

If she is into you then you can suggest some low intensity meet up such as a coffee or meeting at the local mall and so on. Your still in the "online stranger" category so the meet up should not put too much pressure on her. Simply find a suitable time for both of you and then suggest a decent place to meet.

Wechat

Wechat is dynamite if you live in China or any areas with a lot of Chinese women nearby. There are three things you should utilize on Wechat. The first is its ability to translate messages from English to Chinese and vice versa. If you come across a cute Chinese chick and she doesn't speak English don't let that put you off. Take her Wechat. This will allow you to converse with her using the inbuilt translation.

Second thing is the search people nearby function. You can set this to be for females only and Wechat will present you with a list of nearby females. Start messaging them and see who bites the bait.

Third thing is the Wechat moments. This is great for social proof and keeping in contact with girls. Comment on her moments and post cool stuff for her to comment on.

Tantan

This is kind of like the Chinese version of Tinder. Again if your in China or in Chinese speaking areas download it and you will have access to lots of women.

Match.com

Match is a dating website billed as having the most people on. There is a monthly fee involved but with that your more likely to find women who are serious about dating. This would be more suitable if your looking for long term relationships.

Bumble

Bumble is another swipe style app that is similar to Tinder. The major difference is that only women can start the conversation. Having some good photos and a nice profile will help you massively here. There are fewer users here but quality is known to be quite high.

OkCupid

OkCupid is another gold mine of varying types of women. Particularly within the eighteen to thirty-five age range. Although you can still find some Milfs on there. They offer a basic account for free or you can upgrade for a small monthly fee. This will give you more features such as advanced search options.

The Challenge

- Take some great photos
- Create a bio
- Number close five women
- Meet four women
- Close two women

Texting

When you have successfully acquired a girls number it's time to begin texting her. Before you meet up again or go on a date you need to make her comfortable and excited to meet you. It doesn't matter if you had amazing chemistry when you first met her. When you start texting the frame is reset at zero and your back to square one. In fact it might be the very beginning if you literally just asked for her number with no interaction.

Texting is the same as standard game, build comfort, attraction and then seduce. Just because you got her number doesn't mean she is ready to sleep with you. You still have to use your skills otherwise she will get bored and stop talking to you.

Remember to act the way you would in person. Never pretend to be someone you're not. If she thinks your going to be a super extraverted guy and she meets a more intimate guy then she will be disappointed. Being more intimate is fine but just make sure you set the right expectations and be authentic.

If your wondering what you should text a girl then your not alone. So many guys are completely clueless about what to do once they get a girls number. Texting is a completely different form of communication that requires its own set of rules. If you want to have success in your dating life then your going to have to master texting. Think about texting as a quick and useful way to make connections with girls and set up dates.

There are two goals when texting girls.

1. Build rapport and comfort
2. Set up a meet

Timing

Before you even send a first text make sure you actually have her correct number. Confirm that ideally when your with her by sending a short text. This also familiarizes her with your number and initiates the start of a conversation.

After that initial text you can say something like "nice to meet you" or use some kind of joke to the way you met or about your first interaction. For example:

"Great to meet a fellow gym beast" or

"It was fun talking about cakes with you!"

The best scenario is when you set some kind of rough ideas for a future date with her in person. This can lead to much more productive texting with purpose.

Don't wait too long to send the first text to her. These days information moves so fast and you want to stay fresh in her mind. Just as important is the period of time you take to reply to her texts. Quality and high status girls are busy. They will take considerable time to reply to your texts. By default most girls will want to look busy and make you wait. You are also a high status person, so you need to take the time to reply.

If your always instantly replying then it shows her that you don't have much going on in your life. Make her wait and wonder about you. Even if you see her text light up your phone, just wait a while to reply. In some cases you will get into a conversation with her where the texting is going back and forwards. Now that is fine as long as it's moving forwards to a meeting. However, if she takes about twenty minutes to reply to your text and you take two minutes than that looks bad on you. Making her wait is attractive. Being too available presents no challenge to her.

A simple rule you can use is to take as long and preferably a little longer then her to reply. When your not texting her she is going to be wondering about what your doing and why you didn't reply yet.

If you get anxious waiting for her reply just put your phone away and go do something else. That way you will have more outcome independence.

Just because she didn't text you back it doesn't mean she is rejecting you. There could be a number of reasons from a bad mood to being busy. The number one thing you should not do is to send her text after text without her replying. Texting her any more than two unanswered texts in a row is death.

If she doesn't answer your first text that's fine. Maybe wait a few days and then engage her again. If she still doesn't answer just drop it and move on. Make space for someone better in your life.

If you haven't heard from a girl for a while then you can use a standard check in text. This involves a simple greeting, her name, an apology for your silence and that you have been busy. Then request her schedule.
For example:

"Hey Cindy! Sorry I have been so quiet, got a huge project on the go...anyways we should catch up soon. What's your plans this weekend?"

Texting Rules

Lift her up

Fun needs to be the foundation of your texting. Girls are highly emotional so using logic to attract them will fail. Use role playing and games to add fun and humor to your texting. Avoid boring subjects and questions such as "what are you doing?" or "where are you?" Rather be playful and keep her curious about you.

Even if a woman texts you things like "how was your day" avoid engaging in those kind of boring subjects.

She is looking for you to lift her up and is more than likely bored. Whenever this happens come back with something fun and specific such as the following.

Her: "What are you doing?"
You: "I'm plotting my world take over"

Her: "How are you?"
You: "I feel like a champion, just ate two burgers"

Always make sure your texts lift her up. Try smiling when you text her to enforce that. If you struggle to come up with something fun to say put your phone down and come back to it later. Or ask her how the thing she is doing is going. That could be something you talked about when you first met her. Such as her love for chocolate, project at work or new exercise class. Ideally you should connect on things that have emotional attachment with them.

Use smiley faces, gifs, pictures, voice notes and memes to lighten up the texting even more. These also work great to reignite a conversation. It can also help to soften some more direct messages or to put a positive spin on topics. Playfulness is a sign of confidence and outcome independence. This will keep girls addicted to you for positivity.

Challenge

Make her chase you by being a challenge and getting her to qualify herself to you. This all increases her investment for you and makes her want you more and more. Psychologically, the more we feel we have worked for something the more we want it. Tell her your a busy guy.

Question the things she says, but do it in a playful way. Ask her to send you pictures, voice notes and requests. These all are ways to get into compliance with you. Avoid being a nice guy or people pleaser. Strong, alpha men are leaders who do and say whatever they want.

Women will often test you to decide if your worth dating or not. They might send you some rude text, not text back or even cancel on you. If you text back with anger or rudeness then it shows her that your too outcome dependent and not a real alpha. Never be fazed by her tests. Just brush them off or even better, laugh at them.

Get her invested

Women are highly emotional and will go up and down in their feelings for you. Keep her interested in you. There are a number of ways that you can achieve this. Make it look like you live a full and busy interesting life. Instead of saying, "I'm bored" say something like "been a busy day hustling and making plans for world domination." or instead of "not doing much today just the usual" say something like "loving life and excited to get out there into the sunshine". It's way more attractive and uplifting.

Appear to be in demand because it's attractive. Offer her the opportunity to meet with you on your terms. You can say something like,

"Hey, how are you? We haven't talked in a while, I have been super busy lately, but I have some time off this week and would love to hear from you!"

Messages like this show her that you're busy but open the door for her to message you.

Other ways to get her more invested are by using voice texting, pictures and videos. Have her send you pictures or videos of her and voice notes. This will require more effort and investment from her.

Never Text Too Much or try hard

Texting a girl too much will only push her away from you. It provides no challenge to the girl and makes you look needy. To avoid making this mistake follow some simple rules.

- Send her the same amount of texts as she sends you 1:1
- Don't send pointless texts. You don't need to reply to things like "enjoy your night" or "take care". Always let it end with her.
- Keep an abundance mentality and never get hung up on one girl. Texting a lot of girls will help you develop that mentality naturally.

In addition it's also possible to not text enough. If you don't strike while the iron is hot so to speak then it will quickly go cold. If she is responding well and initiating conversation then you are probably doing a good job. All the time her interest and attraction is fading. It's your responsibility to make it happen. Women rarely initiate texting. Take control.

Avoid trying to rush things and make plans way too early on. This is a huge mistake of many guys. Women want to get to know you and become comfortable with you first. This is built up over time.

Remember she must always be more invested than you. Hold back a little and let her fall first. Save the best bits for when you meet her in real and start to develop the relationship.

If she is non responsive just leave it to her. You can keep the number but just move on. She might text you one day, no worries. Sometimes the fact that she doesn't text back is a test in itself. She wanted to know that your confident and outcome independent. For her weeding out the losers is essential. Keep pushing forward.

Never Give Up

The difference between the men who get it and those who don't is persistence. Many guys make the mistake of giving up too easily on the they are texting. If they text a girl and don't hear anything back of receive just a short reply they automatically assume she is not interested and give up. This is a huge mistake. In many cases through persistence low investment numbers can be turned around.

Sometimes she might just be busy, be in a bad mood or not quite sure what to say. Fact is you don't really know. So in this regard let some time pass. Ideally at least a few days. Make a note of the last time you contacted any girls so you don't shoot in too quickly. After a few days or a week you can re-engage her with something light and playful. Send something that compels her to respond. For example:

"I just saw your twin"
"Are you still alive?"

You can also try using open loops, for example:

"Guess what...."
"Oh I see what you are now..."

See if she responds. If not just move on.

Be purposeful

Always be purposeful in your texting, have a reason for texting her. Not just some boredom or because your missing her. Many men often forget the reason why they are texting a girl. They get so wrapped up in the back and forth texting but all of it's going nowhere.

Never lose sight of the big picture. All texting should serve some purpose, that's to either get you laid or out on a date. You need to always keep the interaction moving forward. In that regard your texting should be building comfort and attraction for her to want to meet up with you. Then you need to take responsibility and set up a meeting time and place. If you don't initiate direction and purpose then her interest will begin to fade.

Tune into the signs that she is into you. Some of the ways you can tell when she is ready are when she is responding quickly to your texts and your in a back and forth conversation. Other signals include her statements of interest or when she asking lots of questions about you. Always be thinking of how invested she is.

Spelling & Grammar

Finally, make sure you spelling and grammar is on point. Oxford English isn't necessary here. In fact grammatically perfect texting looks way too polished. At the very least make sure it is readable. If your talking with foreign girls then simplify the language a little.

You can shorten words here and there even if the spelling is incorrect such as taking "g" words at the end of sentences. Ending becomes endin, spelling becomes spellin and so on. Also you can add some extra words on for fun and impact such as. Heyyyy or helloooo. Try no to use too many question marks because according to psychology it looks needy. Never use more than one question mark per text.

In addition try to mirror the way she texts. If she uses emojis, use emojis. Speak her style of language and adjust accordingly. If she is a young student then adjust to that. If she is more mature then adjust to that. If she sends short texts then send short texts back and so on. Always be a little less invested in her than she is you. This is the crux of game.

Texting Her to Meet Up

Arranging a meetup with a woman via texting is a straightforward process. First make sure the texting is going back and forth. If it is you can sometimes call her, but make sure you let her know your going to call first. Say something like, 'lets have a quick call to set it up". Calls will accomplish things much quicker than texting. Some girls will be cool with it others not.

Build some connections with her on things you both like to do and reference the first time you met. This opens up many pathways for potential meets. If you both love tea then you can suggest some local tea shop. Or if you both love the outdoors suggest a walk in the park.

Once you have established similar interests you want to figure out a suitable time for both of you. The best way is to make it sound like you're the one in control who is busy. This can be done by using one of the following examples or a variation of them.

"Hey, I'm pretty busy tonight and tomorrow, but after that I have a few days off, hows your schedule then?"

"Hey, I would love to hang out but my schedule is pretty tight these days, although I am off on Sunday and Thursday...are you fee on those days?"

These examples show her that you are a busy man who values his time. This is attractive and will make her want to spend time with you. Once you figured out times and things to do you can set it.

It's important to note that you should not stop texting her after the date is set. Many women are quite unorganized, they don't use a calendar for appointments and will likely forget your date. When you stop texting her after setting the date the chances of her flaking increase. A simple fun text in between now and the date will keep the spark lit. That could be fun things about your life or commenting on her posts. Keep to the texting rules in this regard.

On the day of the date you should send her a quick text in advance just to confirm it. This will guarantee no flakes. Just say something simple such as

"Hey looking forward to tea tonight! See you at 8".

Use these texting guidelines and you will improve your dating life significantly.

Dates

Before you set up a date you need to have some plans for what to do. The key to dates is to make them fun and interesting. Simply pick an activity that both of you are likely to enjoy whilst giving you a chance to get to know each other more.

When your out on a date make sure you convey a relaxed and fun attitude. The idea of a date is to get to know each other more. If you come with a great attitude then she will reciprocate and it will make the date even better. Keep smiling, make jokes, kino with her and tease her. Stick to lighter topics and use the attractive communication guide. Present yourself as the cool, calm, confident and charismatic guy.

Most men are way too pushy on first dates and try to get sexual right away. Tune into her level of interest to get a feel for where she is. At the same time remain outcome independent. Don't get into any heavy kissing or groping too early because it kills any curiosity. Later she might regret going to fast. Unless she seems really down, in that case bring her home!

Many pick up gurus advocate to move fast on dates. Yes that can get you laid and if she shows the signs then go for it. But long term it is a diminishing return for you to rush girls too much. Remember that one of the key traits of being an alpha is outcome independence. Maybe you don't get laid on that date, no worries. Maybe you do, no worries. You're still the same you. Show the woman your in control of yourself and she will end up chasing you! The more desperate you seem and the more you want it the less chance you have. Remember, the hungry don't get fed.

Limit the first date to a maximum of sixty minutes. That limit on time will also leave her wanting more. Additionally it conveys that you are confident and an in demand alpha male. This makes you way more attractive than the hordes of horny men. If you jump straight into bed with her then you are negligent to her flaws. You might end up severely disappointed and or feeling empty.

The First Date

For the first date a simple meetup at a local bar or coffee shop is fine. Stick to simple, low investment dates that won't break the budget. Also stick to things that allow the conversation to flow. If you involve a few alcoholic drinks that's cool because it will make things a lot more relaxed. When your on the date with her make sure you have plenty of kino and conversations that cover sex and emotions.

Avoid loud places or places that will distract your attention such as bars, restaurants or cinemas. Dinner dates are a well known first date idea but actually they are really bad idea before having sex with a girl. Eating is a turn off for most people. Girls will feel bloated and you will likely have to pay the bill. Plus its way too formal for a first date. If you do go for dinner have a good transition set up such as drinks at your place after. Movies are also a bad idea since you can't talk to her much. Unless you have her over to your place directly. Anyway here a few great ideas for first dates.

- Museum
- Coffee date
- Shopping mall
- Picnic

Wait before you ask her out again

After your first date with a woman wait before you ask her out again. Avoid texting her back and forth right away. Let the dust settle and let her start to wonder about you and again leave space for her to chase you. I know how it goes, you met this awesome girl and your dying to meet her again. To keep that train to love town rolling. But you need to hold back a little bit. Hold back and let her fall. Don't worry she is into you because your an alpha man!

Give her the gift of being a mysterious man by giving her some space. There is no rush. Don't be just another guy chasing her. But at the same time keep the purpose there. Save that for real. Therefore remember the principles of texting again at this stage. Purpose, persistence, challenge and fun. After your first date with her just send a simple text such as:

"Thanks for a fun night zoe :)".

That's all you need to do. If she texts you back, do not reply. Let her text be the last one. Do not ask her to hang out again yet or act needy. For the next few days keep texting to a minimum. Keep it fun, light and always let her be the last text of each conversation. Again it's going back to square one with text game.

After a few days have passed you can ask her to meet up again. State a specific time and activity. For best results I usually offer two times on different days. Assume she is available and do not ask. If she is busy she will likely offer an alternative. If that suits you also then go with it. Or if she asks you out and it suits you, accept it.

For every date and after every date repeat this process of waiting and text game until she commits to being in a relationship with you.

The Second Date

If you haven't slept with her on the first date that's fine because it's good to get to know someone before you jump right into bed with them. They could turn out to be a psycho! Set up a second date if you still like her after the first date. This should be something more fun and intimate. Here are some examples.

- Working out together
- Movies at your place

- Cooking for her
- Making cocktails
- Going to the park

At this point you should be thinking about having sex with her. Choose activities that are close to your home or would be natural to lead to your home. If you go on more than three dates without getting laid then it starts to become a waste of time. Unless the chemistry and sexual vibe is strong. Otherwise move on.

Oh, and if she ever flakes on you, don't make a big deal of it. Just let it go and re-engage one more time if it's right for you. Otherwise move onto new women who are a better match for you.

Sex

Most men are awful in bed, they have no idea what they are doing and have a lack of experience. Howevere in orded to enjoy great relationships of love, passion and intmacy then you need to learn to get good at sex. Learn through the techniques and information outlined in this chapter. Don't be afraid to experiment and try new things out. Experiment with your own variations and get some practice in!

Sexual Attraction

The chances of a woman sleeping with you are connected to how much she thinks about you. If you are the guy she thinks about sexually the most then your chances of having sex with her are increased. This can be confusing to master for most guys since she might seem interested in you but it hasn't progressed to sex yet. This is a result of not turning her on enough. When you master how to turn women on then your results will go through the roof.

For a woman to want to have sex with you, she needs to feel sexual attraction for you. Her sexual attraction is based on what you do and say when your around her. Your conversations and presence should turn her on. The better you are at this, the more attracted she will be to you. Women are like a temperature dial that can be tuned all the way to boiling.

Take responsibility for building attraction, it doesn't happen by chance or magic. You have to take purposeful actions. State that you find her attractive. This conveys confidence and turns women on. Women are mostly in their heads and receiving a positive confirmation from an attractive man is powerfully attractive. But make sure she is clearly attracted to you before you say any compliment. Ideally she would be in your arms and kissing you. Build up sexual tension with flirting and intensity.

There are four factors which will determine the likelihood of you having sex with a new woman.

Judgement

Many women are afraid of being judged for having sex.

- Judged for having sex with somone who they are not in a relationship with.
- Judged for having sex with someone too quickly and so on.
- Fear that her friends with judge her
- Fear that you will judge her
- Her own self judgement

All of this can be difficult for a man to understand since we are often met with praise for our conquests. For women sex is much more emotional and there is more to lose.

To calm her and nullify any judgement you first need to convince her that your not going to judge her. Anytime she brings up the subject of sex listen with an open mind. Allow her to speak in detail and hold back from judging her. This will make her more open to you and more likely to have sex with you because she knows that your a cool guy.

Tell her that you are attracted to women who are liberal. Confirm that with past experiences and stories. Tell her that men and women are equal regarding who they sleep with and should not be judged by it.

Tests

On a conscious and subconscious level women are constantly testing men to discover if they will make a suitable partner or not. Before having sex with you she is likely to test you often. How you respond to those tests will determine your results. She might say things such as:

"You're nice, but nothing is going to ever happen between us,"

"How dare you touch my ass"

"Why didn't you text me back"

The way you deal with her tests is to be cool, calm and collected. Even better if you respond to them in a funny way. This will show her that your a real alpha man who is outcome independent. Responding with nervousness or complying with her will put you right into the friend zone or just another loser guy zone. Hold the frame of being a cool alpha who is outcome independent.

Let's look at some great ways to respond to her tests. Saying these with a deadpan expression and then holding the following silence is dynamite.

"You're nice, but nothing is going to happen between us"
- Good: "Oh well life goes on" and smile (in your mind - haha your gonna get it so bad)
- Bad: "But I like you so much"

"How dare you touch my ass"
- Good: "Shut up you love it" and smile (in your mind - just you wait)
- Bad: "I'm so sorry baby"

"Why didn't you text me back"
- Good: "Awww, did you miss me?" and smile (in your mind - she is so into me)
- Bad: "Please forgive me"

Making it happen

When sex is about to happen make the most of the experience. Enjoy yourself and make her orgasm multiple times. She will be coming back for more and more.

Ambiance

Women are sensitive to their surroundings. Being in the right environment is crucial for amazing sex. At the minimum it should be you and her in an isolated and comfortable place. Yes, you can take her to the toilets and bang her. But for higher quality girls you should have a better place ready.

Set the mood with some nice background music and soft lighting. Make sure the place is clean, comfortable and private. Improve on these things with items such as candles, drinks and soft pillows.

If your in a hotel choose a decent one. Not some ghetto hostel. It can be done but she probably won't come back. If you have none of the above suggest going to her place for drinks.

Sexual Talk

When you are in the right place have the right conversations. Focus on the seductive and sexual topics. Explore her fantasies, tell sexy stories and verbalize your desires. Stay away from boring or everyday subjects. Encourage her to open up.

Kino

Throughout your interaction with a woman you should be applying kino. From the moment you meet it can be things such as checking her hands, tattoos and so on. When you are in a more isolated environment you can start to escalate the kino. Give her a hug, massage her, touch her neck and move in for a kiss.

At the early stages don't touch her private parts just yet. Escalate smoothly and take your time. When you first kiss, be gentle and let your lips brush against each other's. Pause and create some anticipation. Don't just put your tongue in her mouth right away. Let the intensity progress smoothly.

Arouse Her

For us guys all we need to see is a hot, naked woman's body. This enough to arouse most of us! But for women it's much more psychological. All those erotica novels sell like hot cakes because of that. Start priming her mind before you meet up with some naughty texting.

For sex to happen she needs to be attracted to you. This isn't based on looks but more of a desire for you. You also need to make her feel safety which comes from building comfort and connection with her.

Foreplay

It's no secret that women have way more sensitivity to foreplay and experience sex more intensely then men. Valuable time should be spent on foreplay. Ideally you should have her orgasm before you even have sex. This will put her at ease and also take the pressure of you to make her orgasm again during sex. In addition it will probably make it more likely to happen. Plus you will be turned on and dying to bang her!

It would be a huge mistake to assume that the only way to make a woman orgasm is through sex. There are so many studies to prove this.

During foreplay, take your time and undress her, touch her whole body with light touches, soft biting and kisses. Do all of this whilst ignoring her breasts and pussy. This will drive her crazy.

Here are some sensitive areas that you can begin with

- The back of her neck
- The back of her ears, gently bite them
- Her eyes, look deeply into them
- Inner thighs
- Hair, pull it gently

From there start to move towards her breasts. Take off her bra. At the same time take off your shirt. Take her breasts. Suck and gently bite the nipples and around them as you massage them with your hands. Women are super sensitive to their nipples so don't go too hard on them. Vary the intensity as you tune into her verbal and physical cues. If you can tell she is enjoying it spend more time on what your doing.

Whilst your playing with her breasts start to touch her pussy over her underwear. Use your whole hand to gently massage over it. Tease around her pussy, brush your hand around and over it. She will be moaning in anticipation. Take off her underwear. Take a shower together or separately.

Finger her

By now she should be totally naked, horny and wet. Focus on her pussy. Make sure your nails are trimmed and your hands are clean before you do anything else. For the best results have her laying down on her back with you beside her. Begin fingering her.

Massage around the vulva with two or more fingers. The vulva forms the entrance of the pussy and is essentially the whole of it. Do this for around two minutes. Make sure it's wet, if not add lube or saliva to your fingers. Keep making out with her or sucking on her nipples whilst doing this.

Next move up to the clitoris. The clitoris is the pleasure center of the pussy and it can be found at the top of it. It looks like a small hood sticking out. Massage gently around the clitoris in a circular motion and experiment with different movements. Try up and down, circles, diagonal, big and small movements, fast and slow movements. Follow her cues.

Pay attention to the noises and moves she makes. This will signal you to go with what works. By doing this you can make her orgasm quite quickly. Usually it takes an average of fifteen minutes. After this or instead of this you can go down on her.

Going down on her

The skill to be able to go down on a girl is something every man should master. Follow the procedure outlined but do it in your own way as you follow her signals, sounds and body language to guide you.

1. *Avoid her pussy at the beginning*

When your first touching her and doing some light foreplay start to make moves down to her pussy with your mouth. Kiss and gently lick her body all the way down to the pussy. Consciously move around her pussy. Explore her inner thighs, and the edges of her pussy. Blow lightly on her pussy.

2. *Lick and finger*

Start to focus on actually licking her pussy and clitoris. Experiment with different types of licking. Try up and down, side to side, circular and so on. Vary the speed and intensity. Follow her sounds and body signals. Put your finger in and stimulate her.

3. *Keep at it*

Vary your intensity and movements based on her signals. All women are different and will respond to different techniques. The best way is to start slowly and gradually ramp up the intensity. Talk to her whilst you do it. Ask her if she likes it. Keep at what works and you will have her coming in around twenty minutes or less. Then you can bang her really good.

Sex toys

Using sex toys can add spice and lot's of orgasms to your relationships. When you have been seeing and having sex with a girl for a while suggest using sex toys. Or if she suggests them, go with it. You can really have her coming super fast with the aid of sex toys. They will make her wet and dying to bang you even more than before. In turn your sex life will go through the roof!

Sex

One of the biggest myths about sex and women is that men think women are innocent and would not like sex as much as them. This is completely false. Women in fact love sex much more then men but conceal their fantasies because of all the slut shaming out there. Women have more receptors for pleasure than men and can be turned on in many more ways. For women sex is about the entire experience and not just one particular thing.

Contrary to popular belief sex is not like porn. Yes you can get inspired by it but it's completely different from real life. Too much porn will make you insecure about performance and hamper your sex life. The expectations are unrealistic and the stimulus is completely different.

Porn is very one dimensional in the way it portrays sex. There is more than one way to bang a girl than just hardcore sex. Doing that will likely make her sore and unsatisfied. Switch it up between, fast, hard, sensual, loving and so on. Vary it and go with the flow.

After you have made her orgasm from foreplay it's time to move onto sex. Get your condom on (unless you are in a relationship or trust that each other is safe). Make your dick wet and slowly put it inside her pussy. Pay attention to her sensations, be present and take in the whole experience. Make out with her and play with her boobs as you start slowly banging her.

Always be present and totally in the moment during sex. When you first penetrate her just use the tip of your dick for the first few minutes. Build the suspension and slowly put more into her with every stroke.

Take charge of her, be the man. Focus on her sensations and hold yourself back from cumming too quickly. Again be present, in the moment and thoughtless.

Let her know that you're enjoying it. Women are so self concious during sex. Giving her reassurance will put her at ease which increases the chance of her organsiming. Compliment her body, attractiveness and performance. Tell her what you like and what you want more of.

Make noises. This lets her know you're enjoying it. Too many guys are silent. If your just silently grinding her then she has no clue if you are enjoying it or not. Let go of being self conscious and release the sound. Grunt, roar, shout and groan. She will follow your lead and you will have dynamite sex.

Vary up your sexual positions. Again follow her cues. The quickest way to her pleasure is to understand her. Get in her mind with the talking, variance of sexual positions, motions and technique.

When you start sleeping with beautiful women you need to get good at it in order to have them coming back for more. Make sure that she orgasms before you finish. To further help you I have devised a method for having great sex every single time. That could be with your long term partner, friends with benefits or just a one night stand.

The method covers four different characteristics. Combine them and you will blow her mind and make her addicted to having sex with you. It really is that powerful!

Power

It's no secret as to why Fifty Shades of Grey is an international best seller and most of the readers are women. Women love a powerful man who takes control of her in bed. They want to have their arms pinned down whilst you ravage them. They want to be smacked and spanked whilst you bang them. Some of them will even like their hair pulled or enjoy being choked as you penetrate them. Fifty Shades of Grey exhibits this perfectly and taps into female sex psyche.

Now you should make sure the girl is compliant to this before you go about rag dolling her. Start off gently and try some light hair pulling or gentle choking. As you get to know her more, you can start to push things. Tear off her clothes and ravish her, but make sure she is cool with it. If she seems visibly put off by it then pull back. Otherwise continue to dominate her.

Most women will love this. Don't be afraid to unleash the power! Some will be frigid and shy. They might need more exposure to you or they just might not be into that kind of thing. Pay attention and always be in tune to her responses and feedback.

Emotion

Women are extremely sensitive to emotions. Emotions are a hardwire to turning her on. They are authentic, can't be faked and will connect deep within her. That could be positive emotions such as love and intimacy or negative emotions such as anger, shock and surprise. Test each girl to see which she responds well to. One night stands tend to respond better to the negative emotions which will trigger her wild side. Whilst more long term partners will respond better to positive emotions which will trigger her loving and passionate side.

From the very beginning spike her emotions with the things you say and do. Call her a horny little slut whilst you bang her. Or tell her you love her whilst having passionate sex. Observe how she responds. Follow the pathway of which way she responds to. For example if she responds well to positive emotions then caress her, make love to her and say sweet loving things to her whilst you have sex. If she responds well to negative emotions then ravish her as you call her your slut and spike her wild side.

Words aren't the only way to spike emotions. Walk up to her, pin her to the wall and make out with her passionately. This will spike her surprise. Hold her closely whilst you make love or squeeze her hand as you smile at her. This will spike her loving emotions. Emotions will have her addicted to you and coming back for more.

Mix it up

To keep your sex life interesting mix it up. In a relationship couples will often get into a routine way of having sex under the same circumstances and same ways. This quickly becomes very boring and is unlikely to result in much pleasure or an orgasm for her or even you. It's just going through the motions.

If you want to continue having the best sex then you need to mix it up. Try different things, times, places and situations. Stop doing the same things every time. If you always have sex with your woman at night, try doing it in the morning or afternoon. Be spontaneous and surprise her. She might resist at first but push through and blow her mind. If you always start out in missionary, then start with doggy and so on.

Try different positions, speeds, emotions and power. Try starting out just pulling down her skirt and banging her over the kitchen sink. Get creative. Have sex in the shower, in the living room, in the car. Try different places. It's all about mixing it up.

Send her some naughty texts during the day. Spike her emotions and get her lusting to meet you later. Keep her on her toes with all of the variety. Keep making things interesting and experimenting with your sex life. You will be amazed at the life it brings back to your relationships.

Presence

Be in the moment when you have sex and you wil blow her mind. Now this one is difficult to apply. Most of us are so in our heads when having sex. Thinking things like:

"I want to come"
"Has she come yet"
"I wonder if she likes this"
"Am I going to fast"

All of this thinking is creating a wall between both of you having the best sex possible. Instead, let go and be in the moment. This requires you to be one hundred percent into what your doing. Great sex is all about that.

Have an intense presence to your sex. Look into her eyes whilst you penetrate her. Feel all of the sensations, pay attention to your whole body connected to hers. Take all of her in, her sounds, smell, taste and feel. Communicate with her. Tell her you want her to come. Tell her your loving it. Tell her when your going to come.

Cultivate a present mind through the daily practice of meditation and mindfulness. It will make your sex life infintiely better. Little thoughts distract you from the beauty of life and sex. Make her feel like she is the only girl in the world. All you need is to meditate for around twenty minutes a day and you will be able to zen fuck her brains out!

After Sex

Spend time with her after sex. Hold her and talk about how great the sex was. Discuss what you both liked and want more off. Be intimate and vulnerable. Cuddle her, this is really important because she needs to feel validated again. Spend at least fifteen minutes in eachothers arms. Just lay there and be with her. If you see her as a potential girlfriend then go eat with her or have a drink with her somewhere after. This will solidify the relationship in her mind.

Pro tip

Do you want to have stronger erections, last even longer and be able to bang even more? Kegel and kettlebell exercises are your answer. These strengthen your PC muscle which affects sexual performance. It can even help you to delay ejaculation.

Relationships

Relationships are the end goal of dating, attraction and seduction. But being in a relationship doesn't necessarily mean being exclusive with the same woman forever. In modern society that is becoming less likely. But if that's your goal, then that's all good too. At this stage it's important to be aware of and understand the different kinds of relationships and how you can go about setting them up.

Hooking Up

The most basic level relationship is the one night stand / hook up. You meet a girl, sleep with her and never see her again. These are good for a while and great if your a beginner gaining experience. In fact I recommend them if you are lacking in experience. But don't get stuck there. It can quickly become an empty pursuit. If you find yourself continually doing this then your probably not attracted enough to the women your sleeping with or you have some inner self esteem issues that are pushing women away from seeing you again.

Additionally lifestyle plays a huge factor in this. For example a touring DJ or musician is going to be put into this position a lot. But the choice is ultimately yours, stay grounded and aware of your true values. As you gain more experience, try to get to know women more before you sleep with them and make yourself vulnerable.

Hooking up can continue to be fun, especially if you travel and there is no manipulation or games being played. If your in some kind of open relationship then hooking up with girls on the side can be a healthy thing to do. At the end of the day uphold a high standard and treat the women that you hook up with respect. If you want to hook up with a lot of women then night game and online game are your best options.

Friends with benefits

Oftentimes you will meet girls that you find attractive enough to sleep with but on an emotional level they are not quite suitable for a relationship. Men and women both have sexual needs to be fulfilled. Friends with benefits relationships are a great way to fulfill those.

These kinds of relationships usually last upto three months or less. By that point one of you will start to catch feelings or the relationship will fade.

Getting into this scenario first requires you to have sex with a woman. Or you could suggest casual sex arrangements to one of your female friends. Contrary to popular belief and what mainstream media hypnotizes us with you don't need to be really good looking. Women seeking friends with benefits will always prefer some cool guy with good game then a clueless hunk.

Direct communication is a prerequisite for establishing friends with benefits relationships. Be clear about what it is and don't let her fall for any illusions of later relationships. Women are more emotionally attached to sex and can easily fall in love through it. Respect her feelings with honesty and if she wants more but you don't, then let her go. Build trust with her and also make sure she is not expecting more. That relies on finding the right women. Explore the conversation with her. You can still hang out and do friends things together. Treat your female friends just like you would your male friends. Hang out with them and have a good time. It could always lead to more intimacy if you want.

Women don't want you going around bragging about these relationships, so if you can be discreet and non needy then you will have great success. Telling stories is a great way to convey that you will be discreet and non needy. For example the time your housemate starting dating the manager at work. "I knew it all along and everyone kept asking me but I kept my promises. Their secret was safe with me." Stories like this communicate that you don't bend to pressure and you can be trusted to keep secrets.

Open Relationships

An open relationship involves two or more people romantically involved in a relationship making a consensual decision to have non-monogamy. This could involve introducing new sex partners together or seperately. Those new sex partners would typically be non romantic. Most women are presented with two worlds. The friends with benefits world and the monogamous relationship world. But the in-between dynamic that many women don't know about is open relationships.

Open relationships allow for a lot of experimentation, cater for different set of needs and take the pressure off each person. You can have a very successful happy relationship even if you still meet other people occasionally. We all have different sides of wants and needs. It's virtually impossible that one single person will be able to fulfill all of them. Sometimes you might want a girl that's kinky. Other times you might want intellectual stimulation from a girl that knows a lot about business. Or a girl that goes to the gym and so on. There's all these different needs and it's virtually impossible to find all of those in one person. A simpler and more elegant solution is that different people will fulfill different sets of needs that you have. Obviously that works for both sides of the relationship. No double standards and no judgement.

Usually what happens in a conventional, exclusive relationship is that people get comfortable. Maybe they got a little bit fat or they don't dress that well anymore because they became too comfortable. Open relationships will keep both of you on your toes. When you continuously meet other people you will be on top of your life, which is very attractive. Think about anytime you had a relationship that ended. You felt sad and that lasted for a certain amount of time. But then what happens after is you always get better. You start to improve yourself again, you hit the gym again, buy nice clothes go out again meet people and maybe start to do some other hobbies.

In an open relationship you have to really pay attention to your emotions, as you encounter any negativity, jealousy or guilt and so on. Figure out why are you feeling jealous or why are you feeling guilty? Jealousy won't serve you well so try to get rid off it. You don't need to know intimate details of eachothers sex lives but being ok with the idea of it is a fundamental requirement.

A successful open relationship is based on trust and respect. Honesty needs to prevail. To make it work some boundaries need to be defined. Consider the following:

- Are you allowed to become romantically involved with others?
- Are you allowed to have others stay the night in your house?
- Are you allowed to stay the night with others?
- Is it important to know about their sex life?
- How will they meet other people to have sex with?

- Are certain people not allowed? This could be ex partners, friends and so on.
- Will they use protection?
- How often can they have sex with other people?

These are all things to consider. Add more if you feel they are necessary. Once you have set the boundaries, stick to them. They can be discussed later on if the dynamic of the relationship changes.

Approaching the subject can be intimidating, you might fear losing her. But honesty is the best way forward. You don't want to be caught cheating. Begin the conversation by talking about the possibility of open relationships. Before you discuss it have a clear idea of what you're looking for.

Now you should only ever set this up after sex. If you try to set it up before sex it will ruin your chances. Come at it with the attitude of stating your views and being clear about it. Be clear that you enjoy freedom and that monogamy is not for you. For example say something like the following:

"Right now in my life I really want to pursue my career. It means so much to me that I'm not allowing myself to attach myself to any particular type of thing. But what we have is so beautiful that I want to keep it going with you."

Clarity allows her to trust you more. When a man is ambiguous it conveys non trust. If you have shown her that your man that likes her, respects her and that really wants to make her feel special then you can create whatever it is that you want as long as you have clarity around it.

Tell her you value your relationship with her and tell her your opinion on open relationships. You can also mention something like it gives each other more freedom. Accept that she can also see other people. You have to be open about that from the start. If she thinks you're exclusive then that's bad. Give her time to think about it. There is no guarantee she will accept it. But she might leave for a while and come back later on.

Monogamy

Monogamy means you being exclusive to one woman and her being exclusive to you. No side relationships or hookups. For many people a loving relationship is far more rewarding then lot's of casual dating and casual sex. In an exclusive relationship you build trust, authenticity and love. When you fall in love with someone naturally you will want to be only with them. Of course that can change and you might want to transition to an open relationship. But if you want to stay exclusive then there are some great ways to keep the spark going. We discussed many of those in the section on relationships within the female psychology chapter. Here are some more tips.

Many guys who once they discover and develop dating skills fear that when they become involved in an exclusive relationship they will lose that skill. This is not true and you shouldn't fear it. As men we can reproduce until we die. With good nutrition, exercise and personal development we can stay attractive for a long, long time. In fact, men often become more attractive as they age because they build better lifestyles, stronger character and more resources. This is extremely attractive for younger women.

Make your relationship decisions from a place of abundance. Ultimately it's up to you what kind of relationship you want. Avoid lying to yourself and others. If you go around pretending that you want a relationship and really you just want to hook up with a lot of women then your going to disappoint a lot of women and yourself. That's why cheating happens. Have clear, written goals and values that you internalize and honor.

How you approach relationships can cause you a lot of discomfort later on or a happy and pleasurable experience. If you create a relationship out of the fear of being dumped or single then it will usually end in suffering. Case in point I was once dating a very attractive girl who asked me to be exclusive. At that time I really didn't want to but I felt she would leave me if I didn't agree. So I agreed. The result was a lot of dishonesty, me cheating all the time and eventually the relationship ended in disaster.

There is no need to rush into a relationship. Always be screening women in your life for the things you look for. Hold the frame and be the buyer. Negligence can come when you date a really hot woman and disregard her personality flaws.

Set some boundaries for what you expect from each other. Don't fear this. The longer you leave it the less attractive you become and the relationship chances for success diminish. Women want a strong man who can make decisions. If you don't like her texting other guys or partying every night tell her. See how she reacts. Avoid confrontations and instead calmly explore those issues. Ask her how she feels and what she wants. The outcome will be much better for both of you.

If you are in an exclusive relationship always maintain your alpha male character. Many guys become suckers in relationships and become way to compliant. It sounds selfish but in fact women will respect you much more for being this way. Your personal development is more important to any woman. You have to be willing to face losing her. Hold your purpose above that.

Relationships should be fun. When she tries to pull you into drama or tests handle it with fun and indifference. Most of it will be small stuff. There will be serious times and if you have done wrong then man up and apologize to her.

Don't stop gaming and dating her. Tease her, date her, make her chase you and want to be with you. Maintain this dynamic from the start, when you make her feel motivated to be with you she will enjoy it.

In an exclusive relationship never let sex be something your getting from her. This will turn her off and make her use it against you. Again this involves always gaming her and making her want you instead of you being a compliant guy begging for sex. Surprise her with gifts, calls, or texts that show you how much you appreciate her. Keep going on fun dates and having new experiences together. All this will keep the relationship strong and exciting. Create a dynamic where she is excited to have sex with you.

Confidence and outcome independence again should be the pillars throughout your dating journey. They are pivotal in relationships. Never fear being hurt or falling in love. Be confident enough to make yourself vulnerable. Be confident enough to tell her you love her. But don't be besotted by her or make her your world. Again, have your goals and your own life.

If your relationships stop making you happy or is negatively affecting your life then it's time to move on. Open the door for someone better to come into your life. Don't hesitate on doing this. The longer you leave it the harder it gets to break free and to recover.

Conclusion

There's this famous scene in the movie, The Matrix. When Morpheus first introduces Neo to the red pill and the blue pill decision. I have rephrased it somewhat to apply to the knowledge in this book.

"Take the blue pill and you wake up tomorrow with no memory of this book. You go back to your boring life. Watching porn and getting laid with the odd average girl here and there."

"Take the red pill and I show you just how deep this goes. Abundance with women. Dating who you want when you want. Sex, sex and more sex. Multiple relationships. The love of your life."

Never stop learning. There are so many more views on this subject and you should expose yourself to them. Constantly refresh your knowledge. Read this book again and again. Listen to it, take the challenges, take notes and immerse yourself in it.

Different parts will resonate with you at different times in your life. You can skip to those chapters where you happen to be stuck. But don't get stuck in information. Taking action on the information is the number one important thing you can do.

Go out and start approaching women. Get your lifestyle fixed. Start meeting people. Make your life more attractive and more fun. Do the things you want to and not what others expect of you. The women will come and your self esteem will be at its peak. Ready to attract the best women for you,

Master the fundamentals. Conversations, inner game, outer game, meeting women and so on. Challenge yourself to work on the specific things that are holding you back. For example, if you struggle to talk to woman for longer than two minutes then go out and focus on staying there. Or, for example, if your having trouble closing girls then go out and focus on closing them. Find out what your weaknesses are and push past the discomfort. Facing the challenges and overcoming them will make you better. They might recur later on as well. But if you ignore the challenges then you will stagnate. That could be for years. Avoid this and continually check in with yourself to see how your going. Take detailed notes, review them regularly and set your goals, short term and long term.

One of the best ways you can make massive progress is to find a mentor.

There is nothing in this world that could be a better investment than the one in yourself. Hiring a coach could be the best thing you'll ever do. If your interested:

Get in touch with me at: chaseattraction@gmail.com
Or www.darcycarter.com

I would love to hear from you.

Tell me what you learned from this book, and how it has changed your life. Leave me a review or drop me a message.

Yours sincerely

Darcy Carter

Thanks for Reading!

What did you think of, **Dating Advice For Men: Discover What Women Want & Become An Alpha Male Who Easily Attracts & Seduces Women**

I know you could have picked any number of books to read, but you picked this book and for that I am extremely grateful.

I hope that it added at value and quality to your everyday life. If so, it would be really nice if you could share this book with your friends and family by posting to [Facebook](#) and [Twitter](#).

If you enjoyed this book and found some benefit in reading this, I'd like to hear from you and hope that you could take some time to post a review. Your feedback and support will help this author to greatly improve his writing craft for future projects and make this book even better.

I want you, the reader, to know that your review is very important and so, if you'd like to leave a review, all you have to do is click here and away you go. I wish you all the best in your future success!

Please keep in touch with me and updated with me at:

https://darcycarter.com/

Thank you and good luck!

Darcy Carter

Free, Sign Me Up

Buyer Bonus

I want to thank you for your purchase of this book. As a way of extending my thanks I am offering a **free** dating course and two ebooks.

The course is, Attract Women: The Simple Strategy to Attract Women will help you to realize your dating goals much quicker. Whilst the two books, **The Confident New You** & **Make Her Chase You** will help you gain more confidence and success with women.

Here's just a tiny fraction of what you'll discover:

- Smooth ways to ask the girl for her number and have amazing dates, relationships and mind blowing sex.
- Build a lifestyle that will guarantee you success with women
- Where to easily meet women in your city
- How to Look and Feel Your Best
- Keep the conversation going, without appearing awkward
- How to confidently express yourself and captivate attention
- And much more about confidence, relationships and dating

So if you're looking for a simple way to attract women and have more confidence then:

Buyer Bonus 2

Confident Dating, Attract Women with Confidence

Do you feel like you need more confidence when approaching women, asking for their number, or even asking them on dates? If so, then this audiobook is for you!

Including:

- *The Confident New You - Develop Your Confidence and Start Living the Life You Deserve*
- *Make Her Chase You: The Simple Strategy to Attract Women*

So, if you're looking for a simple way to attract women and have more confidence then click the link.

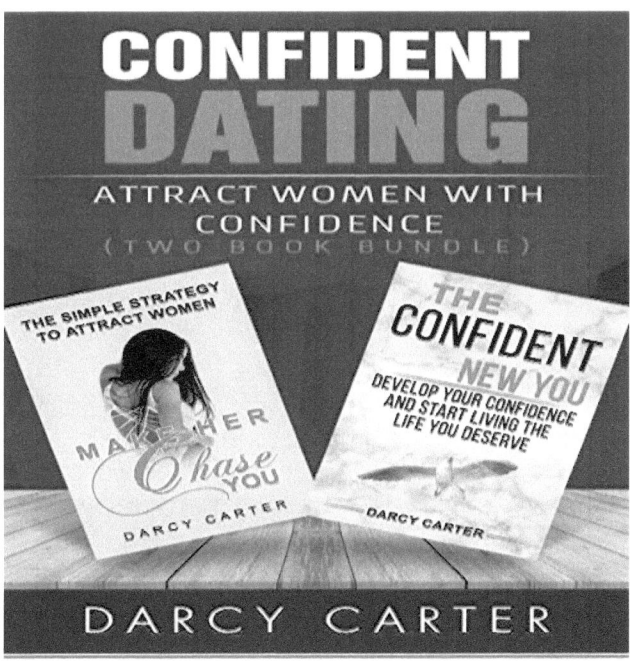

www.ingramcontent.com/pod-product-compliance
Lightning Source LLC
Chambersburg PA
CBHW021107080526
44587CB00010B/426